SIX STEPS TO A LONG-RANGE PRESERVATION PLAN

SIX STEPS TO A LONG-RANGE PRESERVATION PLAN

A Guide for Cultural Heritage Collections

Sherelyn Ogden

ROWMAN & LITTLEFIELD
Lanham • Boulder • New York • London

Published by Rowman & Littlefield
An imprint of The Rowman & Littlefield Publishing Group, Inc.
4501 Forbes Boulevard, Suite 200, Lanham, Maryland 20706
www.rowman.com

86-90 Paul Street, London EC2A 4NE

Copyright © 2025 by The Rowman & Littlefield Publishing Group, Inc.

All rights reserved. No part of this book may be reproduced in any form or by any electronic or mechanical means, including information storage and retrieval systems, without written permission from the publisher, except by a reviewer who may quote passages in a review.

British Library Cataloguing in Publication Information Available

Library of Congress Cataloging-in-Publication Data

Names: Ogden, Sherelyn, author.
Title: Six steps to a long-range preservation plan : a guide for cultural heritage collections / Sherelyn Ogden.
Other titles: Guide for cultural heritage collections
Description: Lanham : Rowman & Littlefield, [2024] | Includes bibliographical references and index. | Summary: "This nuts-and-bolts approach prioritizes needs based on urgency and feasibility to ensure that the best use is made of valuable resources. The result is a practical document that will guide preservation activities and aid in fundraising for years to come"— Provided by publisher.
Identifiers: LCCN 2024008095 (print) | LCCN 2024008096 (ebook) | ISBN 9781538181065 (cloth : alk. paper) | ISBN 9781538181072 (paper : alk. paper) | ISBN 9781538181089 (electronic)
Subjects: LCSH: Cultural property—Protection—Handbooks, manuals, etc. | Historic preservation—Planning—Handbooks, manuals, etc. | Museums—Collection management—Planning—Handbooks, manuals, etc.
Classification: LCC CC135 .O33 2024 (print) | LCC CC135 (ebook) | DDC 363.6/9—dc23/eng/20240315
LC record available at https://lccn.loc.gov/2024008095
LC ebook record available at https://lccn.loc.gov/2024008096

∞™ The paper used in this publication meets the minimum requirements of American National Standard for Information Sciences—Permanence of Paper for Printed Library Materials, ANSI/NISO Z39.48-1992.

Contents

List of Worksheets		vii
Acknowledgments		ix
Preface		xi
Chapter 1	The Nuts and Bolts of Preservation Planning	1
Chapter 2	The Six-Step Methodology	11
Chapter 3	STEP 1 Lay the Groundwork	19
Chapter 4	STEP 2 Describe the Collections	23
Chapter 5	STEP 3 Identify Needs and Actions and Prioritize Them	29
Chapter 6	STEP 4 Schedule Actions	39
Chapter 7	STEP 5 Compile a Record of the Institution's Preservation Accomplishments	47
Chapter 8	STEP 6 Draft the Introductory Information and Prepare the Final Document	49
Chapter 9	A Few thoughts on Implementing the Plan	57
Appendix 1	Using a Long-Range Preservation Plan: My Personal Experience *By Cynthia Engle*	61

Appendix 2 Background on the Hawaiian Historical Society's Long-Range Preservation Plan 63

By Sherelyn Ogden

Appendix 3 Long-Range Preservation Plan 65

Hawaiian Historical Society

Index 131

About the Author 135

List of Worksheets

Figure 2.1	Grid for Selection of Implementation Priorities	14
Figure 2.2	Planning Procedures Checklist	18
Figure 4.1	Description of Collections	25
Figure 4.2	Description of Collections	26–27
Figure 4.3	Description of Collections	28
Figure 4.4	Description of Collections	28
Figure 5.1	Summary of Needs and Prioritized Actions to Meet These Needs	30
Figure 5.2	Summary of Needs and Prioritized Actions to Meet These Needs	32
Figure 5.3	Categories of Need	33
Figure 5.4	Summary of Needs and Prioritized Actions to Meet These Needs	34
Figure 5.5	Summary of Needs and Prioritized Actions to Meet These Needs	36
Figure 6.1	Long-Range Action Plan and Timetable Fiscal Year 2024–2025	40
Figure 6.2	Long-Range Action Plan and Timetable Fiscal Year 2025–2026	41
Figure 6.3	Long-Range Action Plan and Timetable Fiscal Year 2026–2027	42
Figure 6.4	Long-Range Action Plan and Timetable Fiscal Year 2027–2028	43
Figure 6.5	Long-Range Action Plan and Timetable Fiscal Year 2028–2029	44
Figure 6.6	Long-Range Action Plan and Timetable After 2029	44
Figure 7.1	List of Preservation Accomplishments to Date	48
Figure 8.1	Title Page	50
Figure 8.2	Acknowledgments	51
Figure 8.3	Executive Summary	52
Figure 8.4	Table of Contents	53
Figure 8.5	Introduction	54
Figure 8.6	Prepare the Final Document	55

Acknowledgments

This book reflects the generosity and kindness of many colleagues, friends, and other interested parties, and I am grateful to them. They shared their knowledge, experience, and time and provided support and assistance throughout the project. Of course, any errors or omissions are my responsibility. All those who contributed are too numerous to cite individually. Several, however, should receive special recognition.

The foundation of this book is a previous one I wrote while on the staff of Northeast Document Conservation Center: *Preservation Planning: Guidelines for Writing a Long-Range Plan*. Early in this project I sought input on how the new book would relate to the previous one with regard to publication and use rights. I am grateful to Bill Veillette, executive director, and Ann Marie Willer, director of preservation services, Northeast Document Conservation Center, for their help with this. I also appreciate the useful suggestions regarding content made by Elizabeth Boyne, preventive conservator, Princeton University Library, when she was preservation specialist at Northeast Document Conservation Center. Nicole Graybow, director of preventive conservation, Midwest Art Conservation Center, provided additional practical input on audience needs.

Nine beta readers spent hours reviewing all aspects of the manuscript. I greatly appreciate their valuable comments and suggestions. The book is much better because of their considerable effort, and I thank them. They are: M. Susan Barger, consultant and conservation scientist, retired; Bexx Caswell-Olson, director of book conservation, Northeast Document Conservation Center; Michele V. Cloonan, professor and dean emerita, School of Library and Information Science, Simmons University; Rebecca Elder, consultant, Rebecca Elder Cultural Heritage Preservation; Dyani Feige, director of preservation services, Conservation Center for Art & Historic Artifacts; Mario Anthony Gallardo, emergency preparedness consultant, Northeast Document Conservation Center; Lisa Goldberg, consultant and conservator, Goldberg Preservation Services LLC; David Grabitske, assistant society director and museum director, South Dakota State Historical Society; Robert Waller, president and senior risk analyst, Protect Heritage.

I am very grateful to Cynthia Engle, executive director of the Hawaiian Historical Society. She generously granted permission to include the Long-Range Preservation Plan of the Hawaiian Historical Society in this book. In addition, she agreed to write a section (appendix 1) describing her experience using the plan. The Hawaiian Historical Society's plan, along with her informative and heartfelt essay, form an invaluable contribution.

The use of copyrighted information is gratefully acknowledged. Bill Veillette, executive director, Northeast Document Conservation Center, generously granted permission to use material from *Preservation Planning: Guidelines for Writing a Long-Range Plan*. I thank him. I also thank the Association of Research Libraries for permission to publish a grid from *Preservation Planning Program: An Assisted Self-Study Manual for Libraries* by Pamela W. Darling with Duane E. Webster, expanded 1987 edition (Washington, DC: Association of Research Libraries, Office of Management Studies, 1987). Thanks to Mary Lee Kennedy, executive director, and Kaylyn Groves, director, Member Communications, for making this possible.

I acknowledge the many people who contributed to *Preservation Planning: Guidelines for Writing a Long-Range Plan.* I especially thank Theresa Rini Percy, who created the fictional Daniel J. Dial Clock Museum for that book, which I have used again in this book. Her insight and sense of humor are greatly appreciated.

Several people should be acknowledged for the special assistance they provided. Ann Marie Willer introduced me to appropriate beta readers on the staff of Northeast Document Conservation Center. Michele V. Cloonan put me in touch with the book's publisher. Colin D. Turner, executive director, Midwest Art Conservation Center, provided contact information for regional centers. Thomas Clareson, project director and senior consultant, Digital and Preservation Services, Lyrasus, provided information on that organization. Susan Feller, president and CEO, Association of Tribal Archives, Libraries and Museums, made it possible for me to speak at the association's annual conference and obtain important feedback from participants. Others who assisted with various technical details are: Fun Fun Cheng, executive office and administrative specialist, University of Minnesota Extension; Barbara Dunn, retired administrative director and librarian, Hawaiian Historical Society; Brittany Keefe, marketing and communications director, Young Dance; and Helen Wong Smith, archivist for University Records, University of Hawaii.

I am grateful to Rowman & Littlefield Publishers for accepting this book for publication and to Charles Harmon, executor editor, for guiding me smoothly through the publishing process. Thanks also to Erinn Slanina, associate acquisitions editor and Lauren Moynihan, assistant acquisitions editor. I appreciate their polite and prompt response to my endless questions.

Finally, I thank my friends who patiently listened to my concerns and supported me throughout.

Preface

The number of collections-holding cultural heritage institutions that have had preservation assessments has increased substantially over the years. Thousands of assessments have been funded through federal and state initiatives, while national, regional, and local organizations have subsidized countless more. Unfortunately, the staff of institutions often find themselves overwhelmed by the vast amount of information supplied in the assessment reports and are unable to process it effectively. They do not know where to begin or how to move forward. *Six Steps to a Long-Range Preservation Plan* is intended to assist with this.

The purpose of this book is to help staff convert the information in assessment reports into a plan of action by proceeding through six easy-to-follow steps. The methodology is straightforward and practical. The result is a long-range preservation plan that will facilitate implementation of the recommendations made in assessments, serve as a roadmap for the care of an institution's collections for years to come, and be a formal document equivalent to and in concert with other key management tools in the institution.

Chapter 1 opens with a discussion of preservation planning and the role that preservation assessment plays in it. This is followed by a comparison of generating an assessment in-house versus hiring an outside consultant. The chapter concludes with suggestions for funding and assistance. Chapter 2 introduces each step of the planning methodology. It explains the prioritizing process, which is central to sound planning, and lays out the use of worksheets, which are instrumental to the methodology. Chapters 3 through 8 provide detailed instructions for each of the six steps in drafting a plan and illustrate the use of different worksheets. Chapter 9 offers a few thoughts on implementing and updating the plan once it is drafted. Three appendixes provide additional information.

Every effort has been made to present the methodology as clearly and succinctly as possible. Examples from real situations in a variety of unnamed institutions are provided to clarify instructions. Likewise, helpful tips based on my experience are scattered throughout the book. A variety of worksheets in various stages of completion are also included to illustrate each of the six steps. These worksheets are based on the fictional Daniel J. Dial Clock Museum, located at 55 Tick Tock Road in Spring Valley, Connecticut. It is envisioned as a small nonprofit educational institution with collections that consist of the Archives, Material Culture, Research Library, and Visual Materials.[1] Finally, the long-range preservation plan for the Hawaiian Historical Society appears in its entirety in appendix 3 as a valuable example of an actual plan for a small institution. It has been redacted for security purposes.

Six Steps to a Long-Range Preservation Plan is based on my fifty years of experience working in the field of cultural heritage preservation as a conservator, consultant, and administrator. Having conducted over one hundred assessments and consulted extensively for a variety of institutions, I know firsthand the challenges faced by staff in meeting preservation needs. My years of experience have helped me develop practical solutions to problems and instilled in me the importance of setting priorities to meet goals in the most effective manner. This book complements a previous one I produced—*Preservation Planning: Guidelines for Writing a Long-Range Preservation Plan*. While much of the information is the same, it is presented here in a more accessible way. Also, since writing that book, I have had the opportunity to use it in practice. The methodology proved to be sound, but I think a less comprehensive approach would be easier for users to follow. The methodology introduced here is a streamlined version of the previous one with a simplified prioritizing process and more reliance on worksheets rather than narrative to present information in the final document.

Although the methodology was developed initially for small and emerging museums, it has proven in practice to be appropriate for use by cultural heritage institutions of all types and sizes, such as libraries, archives, historical societies, fine arts museums, and the cultural centers of indigenous people. This book's intended audience is the staff of institutions that have had an assessment and now need assistance taking the next steps to produce a long-range preservation plan. This book aims to help them carry out the planning process without the need for additional outside consultation. It is intended for the person who does *not* have experience drafting a long-range plan and knows little about the process. The hope, however, is that those who *are* experienced will also find it useful.

Technical terminology and jargon are kept to a minimum. A few terms, however, are unavoidable, and they should be defined as used in this book. The term *preservation* refers to "the protection of cultural property through activities that minimize chemical and physical deterioration and damage and that prevent loss of informational content [and intangible value]. The primary goal of preservation is to prolong the existence of cultural property."[2] The term *conservation* refers to: "the profession devoted to the preservation of cultural property for the future. Conservation activities include examination, documentation, treatment, and preventive care, supported by research and education."[3] The term *preservation assessment* refers to an evaluation of the policies, practices, and conditions in an institution that have an impact on the preservation of the institution's collections. A preservation assessment identifies risks to the collections. It "describes the problems that affect the preservation of collections, analyzes the causes of these problems, and suggests a plan of action."[4] Over the years several terms have been used interchangeably to refer to this type of assessment. As used here it has the same meaning as *needs assessment, risk assessment, conservation assessment,* and *Collections Assessment for Preservation (CAP) survey*. The pronoun *you* is used throughout to address the one or more individuals who are participating in the process of drafting the plan. It is intended to address a variety of audiences. It can be the director or a board member in a small institution, a curator or conservator in a large one, or an elder in a cultural center. It can also be a group of people who are working together as a team to produce the plan. The adjective *indigenous* refers to the people inhabiting a land from the earliest times and includes American Indian, Native Hawaiian, Alaskan Native, and all other native peoples everywhere. The noun *institution* refers to the collections-holding entity for which the plan is being drafted. It can be a library, archives, historical society, museum, or the cultural center of indigenous people.

You may notice some repetition in this book. It is intentional. Certain points bear repeating, no matter how mundane and seemingly obvious. Also, this book is not perfect, nor do I claim to have the definitive methodology for preservation planning. Suggestions for improvements are welcome as the methodology is followed and experience gained. The aim of *Six Steps to a Long-Range Preservation Plan* is to aid the staff of cultural institutions in moving forward with implementation of the suggestions in their preservation assessments. I hope this practical, worksheet-based, do-it-yourself approach will have relevance in these times of increasingly sophisticated artificial intelligence and serve the purpose intended.

Notes

1. The content of these worksheets was written by Theresa Rini Percy when she was the director of the Emily Williston Memorial Library and Museum in Easthampton, Massachusetts, and updated by Sherelyn Ogden for this publication. Any resemblance to an actual museum is coincidental. Ms. Percy's valuable contribution is greatly appreciated.

2. "Conservation Terminology," American Institute for Conservation, accessed January 3, 2023, Conservation Terminology (culturalheritage.org).

3. Ibid.

4. Sara Wolf Green, ed. *The Conservation Assessment: A Tool for Planning, Implementing, and Fundraising* (Marina del Rey, CA, and Washington, DC: Getty Conservation Institute and National Institute for the Conservation of Cultural Property, 1990), 2.

Chapter 1

The Nuts and Bolts of Preservation Planning

Preservation is an integral part of the mission of collections-holding institutions. Leading professional organizations for these entities endorse this and include a prominent statement regarding preservation in their codes of ethics and values.[1] Planning for preservation, however, is much work and takes time. You may question why to do it. The answer is that it is a means to an end. It is the most efficient way to preserve the collections in your care, saving time and money in the long run. This chapter introduces you to the planning process, the plan itself, and the preservation assessment. The purpose of the chapter is to provide you with the background for what follows in the rest of the book and to supply you with the practical information you need to carry out the planning process.

The Process and Plan

Preservation planning is a process that determines general and specific collections care needs, establishes priorities, defines a course of action, and specifies necessary resources for implementation. It identifies the actions an institution can take and those it probably cannot take so that you are able to allocate resources appropriately.

The result of the planning process is a written, long-range preservation plan. It is a living document, updated regularly, that provides a snapshot of preservation at a given moment in time. This document can help you in several important ways:

- It lays out a course of action to follow in meeting your needs in a logical, efficient, and effective manner over a set period of time.
- It maintains continuity and consistency in your preservation program over time.
- It validates the role of preservation, helping to make it an equal partner with other functions of your institution, such as acquisitions and interpretation.
- It aids in securing necessary resources to support preservation.
- It provides a written record of your institution's past, current, and future preservation activities.

- Preservation planning is a process that leads to the most effective use of an institution's resources to meet its collections care needs.
- A long-range preservation plan is the written document that results from the planning process. It includes an action plan and timetable—a list of prioritized actions to take over a specific period to meet collections care needs.

The most practicable plans have three characteristics in common. First, they are drafted within the same frame of reference that is used for all collections' policies and plans, the institution's mission statement. They flow from the mission statement and are understood and implemented within its parameters. This enables them to dovetail with other key management tools in the institution. Second, they include all the institution's collections. This is vital for developing a complete understanding of long-term priorities and for linking preservation activities to other strategic planning agendas. Finally, they are realistic. A document that is outside the ability of an institution to implement and sustain is not useful. While it needs to include all recommendations, the plan should focus on those that can be accomplished with existing or obtainable resources.

What the Plan Looks Like

The layout of a plan that is suggested in this book was developed in collaboration with the staff of cultural institutions who have written and used long-range plans. It reflects their experience and is intended to produce a logical and comprehensive tool. It consists of the following sections, which are described in detail later.

- The *Title Page* identifies the document.
- The *Table of Contents* shows the layout of the document at a glance.
- The *Acknowledgments* recognizes the development team and others who contributed to drafting it, including funders.
- The *Executive Summary* provides a brief description of the institution, its preservation commitment, and a synopsis of the plan's findings. This section is formatted to be separated from the rest of the plan and used as a separate document, for example, in support of funding applications.
- The *Introduction* includes the institution's mission, a brief history of its preservation activities, the purpose of the plan, an explanation of any collections excluded from the plan, and a description of how the plan is organized.
- The *Long-Range Action Plan and Timetable* lists all the prioritized actions needed by the institution scheduled over a multi-year period. It includes the resources required and the means of implementation. This is the core of the plan. This section is also formatted so that it can be separated from the rest of the plan and used independently.
- The *List of Preservation Accomplishments to Date* records by year the preservation activities the institution has accomplished. Like the *Executive Summary* and *Long-Range Action Plan and Timetable*, this section is formatted so that it can be separated from the rest of the plan and used as a separate document. It exemplifies progress and is useful in fundraising.
- The *Description of Collections* describes individually every collection included in the long-range plan. This information, which is critical to the prioritizing process, includes: a description; the size or volume; the value, rarity, and provenance; the significance to the institution/reason for preserving the collection; the condition; the kind and amount of use; the length of time the collection should be preserved; the form in which the collection should be preserved; any special cultural considerations; and risk factors of note.
- The *Summary of Needs and Prioritized Actions to Meet these Needs* lists all the institution's preservation needs, the actions and resources required to meet them, and the priority of each action.

- The *Appendixes* vary depending on the institution. They include information directly related to the plan or useful in its implementation. Examples are a list of actions requiring outside funding or a list of projects for interns.

An example of a plan that follows this layout, in general, is provided in appendix 3. Produced for the Hawaiian Historical Society, it is typical for a small to midsized institution. An example of one for a large complex institution is that for the Minnesota Historical Society. It includes abundant information and is appropriate mainly for large institutions with well-established conservation programs. It is available for view on the institution's website at https://mnhs.gitlab.io/archive/conservation/www.mnhs.org/preserve/conservation/reports/2012longrangeplan.pdf.[2]

The Preservation Assessment and Report

A plan is built on the needs of an institution and the actions required to meet these needs. This information is provided in preservation assessments. These are essential to preservation planning and are carried out before a plan is drafted. Many institutions have only one assessment that addresses the needs of all the collections in general terms. Others with numerous diverse collections and complex planning needs may require additional assessments that address particular problems or the needs of specific parts of collections or types of materials.

Since assessments are the foundation of preservation planning, having one that meets your needs is critical. A useful assessment evaluates an institution's policies, practices, and overall environment that affect the preservation of the collections. It addresses the general condition of the collections, what is needed to improve that condition, and how to preserve the collections long-term. It identifies specific preservation needs, recommends actions to meet these needs, and prioritizes the actions based on the level of risk to which the collections are subject and how urgently the action is needed. It is important to note that the building in which the collections are housed is often a part of the collections. This is the case with a historic or architecturally significant structure. In this instance, the actions required to preserve the building, as well as the collections it houses, are considered.

This information is recorded in a formal assessment report. The rationale for recommendations that are made and priorities that are ascribed is stated in the report. Resources that are available to accomplish the recommendations are suggested. The report is written in clear, direct language and is formatted so that information can be easily located and extracted from it. The report is the tool you will use when drafting your preservation plan. It should contain the information you need in plain language and in an easily accessible form.

Outside Consultants Versus In-House Staff

The preservation assessment can be conducted by outside consultants or by qualified in-house staff. Both have advantages and disadvantages to consider before deciding which to choose. It should be noted here that outside consultants can also be used to assist you with drafting the long-range plan once you have the assessment report(s). Consultants, however, cannot carry out the entire planning process. They can facilitate it, but you need to devote the time and effort required for the decision-making that can only be done by in-house staff.

Outside Consultants / Advantages

- Consultants may be more experienced than anyone in your institution. They may have conducted numerous assessments and dealt with a variety of diverse situations. Also, they may be more aware of outside resources that would enable projects to be accomplished. This gives them a broader, more comprehensive base for making recommendations.
- Consultants may be specialists in a particular area or type of collection. This is also useful in making recommendations.
- Consultants usually come without preconceptions and biases and usually can see situations objectively. They should not bring a personal agenda to the assessment and should be less biased than in-house staff.
- Consultants can say things that may be interpreted as critical without fear of being penalized. Thus, they are more likely to point out situations that need to be changed, even if the change is an unpopular one. Likewise, they are not limited or hampered by the political situation of an institution.
- Often, outside consultants are perceived to have more credibility with the staff and administration, even if this is not justified. Consultants are viewed as authorities.
- Occasionally, outside consultants rather than in-house staff are required by funders to support grant requests.
- Perhaps the most significant advantage of using outside consultants is that they have the time to do the job. They can be scheduled to come at a certain time and be expected to produce a report by a specific date.

Outside Consultants / Disadvantages

- Consultants do not know the history or institutional framework in which situations exist. They are unfamiliar with institutional traditions and idiosyncrasies and, as a result, may make unrealistic or out-of-scope recommendations for a particular institution.
- Consultants' time on-site is limited. The only information they have is what staff tell or show them during the site visit. If staff forget something, consultants may not have all the information they need or the chance to observe a situation firsthand.
- The staff time required to work with consultants may be an issue, especially for small to medium-sized institutions that rely on daily attendance to maintain operating costs. Staff may not be able to take time away from their scheduled job duties to facilitate a site visit.
- Hiring consultants typically requires an outlay of money for their fees. The funds may not be available. This makes consultants seem more expensive even though, in reality, staff may cost as much, or even more, when their salary is considered.

In-House Staff / Advantages

- Staff members know an institution's values and functions and understand the institutional framework and background of existing situations. For this reason, they may be able to make more realistic recommendations than outsiders.

- Staff tend to know where all the collections are housed, the peculiarities of the storage spaces, and how the facilities work. They also are more familiar with various management policies, or lack of them. This enables them to work faster and to make more appropriate recommendations.
- Staff may be more thorough, if there are no limitations on their time, compared to outside consultants whose time is limited.
- Using in-house staff avoids an additional cash expense; an outlay of money is not required. This makes their work seem less expensive, although it may cost as much or more when their salary is considered.

In-House Staff / Disadvantages

- Staff members come with their own prejudices and agendas, which may cloud their interpretation of situations, limit their ability to reframe issues and identify novel solutions, and influence their recommendations.
- It is more complicated for in-house staff to be agents of change than it is for outsiders. In-house staff may be reluctant to recommend certain changes because of the negative impact this may have on themselves or others. Also, they may be reluctant to recommend a change because they assume, based on previous experience, that changes will not be made.
- In-house staff may take longer than consultants to produce a plan or report, especially if they are required to carry out their regular job responsibilities simultaneously.
- The administration may view in-house staff as not having the same level of expertise and knowledge as consultants, even if this is not true. Staff members may not have as much perceived credibility.

Sources of Assistance

Sources of assistance—financial, professional, and informational – are available. The following list is not exhaustive. It is intended only to get you started on your search for help.

For *funding* for preservation assessments check these programs.

- The National Endowment for the Humanities (NEH)
  https://www.neh.gov/grants/listing
  - Preservation Assistance Grants for Smaller Institutions
  - Humanities Collections and Reference Resources Grants (HCRR)
- The Institute of Museum and Library Services (IMLS)
  https://www.imls.gov/grants/grant-programs
  - Collections Assessment for Preservation (CAP)
  - Inspire! Grants for Small Museums
  - Museums for America
  - Native American Library Services: Basic Grants
  - Native American Library Services: Enhancement Grants
  - Native Hawaiian Library Services
  - Native American/Native Hawaiian Museum Services

- For funding possibilities for assessments of archival records, check with your state's State Historical Records Advisory Board (SHRAB). SHRABs are represented by the Council of State Archivists (CoSA).
  https://www.statearchivists.org/
- For funding possibilities for assessments in small local historical organizations contact the Field Services Alliance (FSA).
  https://aaslh.org/communities/field-services-alliance/
- For funding possibilities in your area, check with local cultural institutions and preservation organizations and consult the websites of regional conservation centers (see below).

For *do-it-yourself help* conducting in-house assessments see the following resources.

- *The Conservation Assessment: A Proposed Model for Evaluating Museum Environmental Management Needs (1999)* is produced by The Getty Conservation Institute (GCI). It is for museums and is available on the GCI website.
  https://www.getty.edu/conservation/
- *Assessing Preservation Needs: A Self-Survey Guide* is a publication of the Northeast Document Conservation Center (NEDCC). It is for library and archival collections.
  https://www.nedcc.org/assets/media/documents/apnssg.pdf
- *Archives Assessment and Planning Workbook* is produced by the Society of American Archivists. It covers all aspects of archives work with a section devoted to preserving archival and manuscript holdings.
  https://www2.archivists.org/sites/all/files/ArchivesAssessPlanWkbkAug2010.pdf
- *A Preventive Conservation Calendar for the Smaller Museum* is produced by the International Centre for the Preservation and Restoration of Cultural Property (ICCROM). It is a practical introduction to preventive conservation in museums that helps the user identify threats to collections and schedule appropriate actions.
  https://www.iccrom.org
- *Standards and Excellence Program for History Organizations (STEPS)* is a professional development initiative of the American Association for State and Local History (AASLH) that is geared toward small- to mid-sized organizations. It is broader than just preservation and includes all policies and practices.
  https://www.aaslh.org/professional-development/steps/
- *Museum Assessment Program (MAP)* is supported through a cooperative agreement between the Institute of Museum and Library Services (IMLS) and the American Alliance of Museums (AAM) and is intended to help small and mid-sized museums. Like *STEPS*, it is broader than just preservation and addresses organizational management and operation as well.
  https://www.aam-us.org/programs/accreditation-excellence-programs/museum-assessment-program-map/
- *Benchmarks 3.0* is a product of the National Conservation Service, a British not-for-profit membership organization. It is a self-assessment checklist that establishes realistic goals for managing the conservation of heritage collections in museums, libraries, and archives.
  http://www.ncs.org.uk/benchmarks3.php

- *Preservation Self-Assessment Program (PSAP)* is produced by the University of Illinois Library. It is intended to help collections managers prioritize efforts to improve the condition of collections.
  https://psap.library.illinois.edu
- *RE-ORG Method* is produced by the International Centre for the Study of the Preservation and Restoration of Cultural Property (ICCROM). It is a tool intended to help museum staff regain control of their collections in storage.
  https://www.iccrom.org/publication/re-org-method-reorganize-museum-storage
- *Digital Preservation Assessment Handbook* and *Digital Preservation Peer-Assessment* are produced by the Northeast Document Conservation Center (NEDCC). Together they provide a framework for all components of a digital preservation assessment and the next steps for long-term access to these collections.
  https://www.nedcc.org/preservation-training/digital-preservation-assessment-training

For *consultants* who can conduct preservation assessments and help draft long-range plans refer to the following sources.

- *Find A Professional*, produced by the American Institute for Conservation (AIC).
  https://www.culturalheritage.org/about-conservation/find-a-professional
- *Preferred Vendors List*, produced by the Association of Tribal Archives, Libraries, and Museums (ATALM).
  https://www.atalm.org
- The Field Services Alliance (FSA) for consultants for small local historical organizations.
  https://aaslh.org/communities/field-services-alliance/
- The Directory of Archival Consultants, produced by the Society of American Archivists (SAA).
  https://www2.archivists.org/consultants

Regional conservation centers offer *consulting services* and a variety of resources *(workshops, webinars, publications)* on preservation assessments, preservation planning, and funding opportunities. They are listed below.

- Balboa Art Conservation Center
  1649 El Prado
  San Diego, CA 92101
  Tel: 619-236-9702
  https://www.bacc.org
- Conservation Center for Art & Historic Artifacts
  264 South 23rd Street
  Philadelphia, PA 19103
  Tel: 215-545-0613
  https://www.ccaha.org
- Intermuseum Conservation Association
  2937 W 25th St 2nd floor
  Cleveland, OH 44113
  Tel: 216-658-8700
  https://www.ica-artconservation.org

- Midwest Art Conservation Center
  2400 3rd Avenue South
  Minneapolis, MN 55404
  Tel: 612-870-3120
  https://www.preserveart.org
- Northeast Document Conservation Center
  100 Brickstone Square
  Andover, MA 01810
  Tel: 978-470-1010
  https://www.nedcc.org
- Williamstown Art Conservation Center
  225 South Street
  Williamstown, MA 01267
  Tel: 413-458-5741
  www.williamstownart.org
  and
  6000 Peachtree Road
  Atlanta, GA 30341
  Tel: 404-733-4589
  www.williamstownart.org

Another source of *consulting services* is the following.

- LYRASIS, a non-profit membership organization, provides consulting services that include assessments and planning for all sorts of cultural heritage and arts organizations worldwide.
  https://www.lyrasis.org

Other resources you may find helpful include the ones below.

- The Association of Tribal Archives, Libraries, and Museums (ATALM) is an international non-profit organization that maintains a network of support for indigenous programs, provides culturally relevant programming and services, and administers grant funding initiatives. It is a rich source of information and assistance for indigenous people.
  https://www.atalm.org
- *Connecting to Collections Care* is a program of the Foundation for Advancement in Conservation (FAIC) and is funded by the Institute of Museum and Library Services (IMLS). It provides resources, professional development opportunities, and support for collections care to all types of small to mid-sized cultural institutions. Its archive has almost two hundred webinar recordings and hundreds of resources including items about preservation assessments and planning.
  https://connectingtocollections.org/

To reiterate, this list is not exhaustive. You will discover many additional helpful resources as you undertake your search.

Notes

1. "Code of Ethics," American Library Association, accessed January 4, 2023, Professional Ethics | Tools, Publications and Resources (ala.org);

"Core Values," Society of American Archivists, accessed January 4, 2023, SAA Core Values Statement and Code of Ethics | Society of American Archivists;

"Code of Ethics for Museums," American Alliance of Museums, accessed January 4, 2023, AAM Code of Ethics for Museums—American Alliance of Museums (aam-us.org);

"Mission," American Institute for Conservation, accessed January 4, 2023, Association (AIC) (culturalheritage.org);

"Mission," Foundation for Advancement in Conservation, accessed January 4, 2023, Foundation (FAIC) (culturalheritage.org);

"Memorandum of Association," accessed January 4, 2023, the Companies Act, 1948 (iiconservation.org).

2. "Long-Range Preservation Plan," Minnesota Historical Society, accessed August 18, 2023, https://mnhs.gitlab.io/archive/conservation/www.mnhs.org/preserve/conservation/reports/2012longrangeplan.pdf.

Chapter 2

The Six-Step Methodology

Six Steps to a Long-Range Preservation Plan is intended to lead you progressively and methodically through six steps that will help you draft a plan. Each step is covered in detail in the following chapters. This chapter is meant only to introduce you to the process so you know what to expect.

The Six Steps

STEP 1. Lay the Groundwork

Carry out the preparatory tasks: obtain administrative sanctioning and staff support; assign a team; establish a timetable; settle on authorship and language of the document; and gather and review existing documents.

> The planning process is straightforward: identify needs → identify actions to meet needs → prioritize actions → schedule actions.

STEP 2. Describe the Collections

Identify and describe each collection included in the plan and record the information relevant to its preservation. This forms the section of the plan called *Description of Collections*.

STEP 3. Identify Needs and Actions and Set Priorities

List the needs and the actions required to meet them. Then prioritize the actions by assigning a value of high, medium, or low to each one. This forms the section of the plan called *Summary of Needs and Prioritized Actions to Meet Needs*.

STEP 4. Schedule Actions

Schedule actions for implementation in a logical order over a period of years. This forms the section of the plan called the *Long-Range Action Plan and Timetable*, which is the core of the preservation plan.

STEP 5. Compile a Record of all the Institution's Accomplishments

Record the preservation actions the institution has achieved thus far. This forms the section of the plan called the *List of Preservation Accomplishments to Date*.

STEP 6. Draft the Introductory Information and Prepare the Final Document

Draft the *Title Page, Acknowledgments, Executive Summary, Table of Contents,* and *Introduction*. Pull all the sections of the plan together into one document.

Prioritizing Is Essential

As you understand by now, a plan is based on the preservation needs of an institution and the actions required to meet them. Once the actions are identified, the order in which they are carried out is determined. This is prioritizing, and it is central to sound planning. Establishing priorities ensures that optimal use of resources is made.

Criteria for Prioritizing

In her manual on preservation planning for libraries, Pamela Darling describes three criteria that are central to prioritizing—impact, feasibility, and urgency. These criteria are relevant for all types of collections, not just those held by libraries. The first is impact, the extent to which an action contributes to the preservation of the institution's collections. Darling characterizes high-impact actions as ones that dramatically improve the condition of materials, substantially decrease the rate of their deterioration, or enhance current preservation activities.[1] To evaluate impact, think about the degree to which implementing a specific action will help reduce damage and loss to collections. The greater the impact the higher an action's priority. As an example, consider the installation of a building-wide environmental control system. This would contribute to the preservation of every item in the building and thus be of high impact and a high priority.

However, the feasibility of implementing an action also needs to be considered. Actions vary in the amount of time and resources required to implement them. Some are easy to implement, while others are impossible. Some of the factors to look at include sustainability, financial implications, staffing levels and expertise, and policy and procedural changes. The environmental, social, and political feasibility of various actions also must be realistically evaluated. If it is not likely that you can implement an action, it may be given a low priority even if its impact is high. Consider again the example of an environmental control system. For a small institution on a limited budget that relies primarily on admissions and small donations for its survival, installation of such a system would be financially out of the question. Additionally, the mechanical systems in the building probably would not be able to accommodate a new complex system. Even though the impact would be high, implementation would likely be impossible and the priority low.

Another criterion is the urgency of the action. Darling explains that an action can be regarded as urgent if waiting to implement it could cause immediate problems or would mean bypassing an opportunity.[2] All other factors being equal, those actions requiring immediate implementation would be given the highest priority. For example, an institution lacking an emergency response plan is at high risk of serious damage to the collections should a natural or other disaster occur. Additionally, certain funding agencies require that institutions have a plan in place before they consider funding preservation projects. Preparing an emergency response plan would be considered urgent and of highest priority.

Additional factors influential in prioritizing have to do with the collections themselves. These include the size or volume of a collection; its value, rarity, or provenance; the reason for preserving it; its condition; its use; the length of time it should be preserved; the form in which it should be preserved; special cultural considerations; and risk factors of note. This information is recorded in the *Description of Collections*. For example, rehousing an archival collection that is central to an institution's mission in acid-free folders and boxes would be a high priority. If, however, the collection was outside the institution's mission and slated to eventually be deaccessioned, its priority would be low. In this instance, the length of time the collection is being retained is significant in assigning the level of priority. In another example, the conservation treatment of items that have high monetary value but are rarely used would be of lower priority than that of items that are of less monetary value but heavily used. Here the level of use is an influential factor in assigning a value of priority.

A device that illustrates that some actions merit more attention than others was developed by Darling and is shown in a modified form in figure 2.1. Even though this device was intended for use by libraries in the 1980s, it remains relevant today for cultural institutions of all sorts. The impact and feasibility of each action are plotted on a grid. The high-impact actions that can be implemented with relatively little difficulty are placed in box #1. Those that have high impact but are difficult to implement go in box #3. Those actions that are not difficult to implement but will have little impact go into box #2. Those actions that are difficult to implement and have little impact go into box #4.

Darling explains that the actions in box #1 probably warrant the highest priority since they can be easily accomplished and will have significant impact. Those in box #4 often can be postponed or even disregarded because they achieve little while requiring great effort. Many of those in box #2 also can be eliminated because they accomplish comparatively little, though some may be worthwhile because they are easy to do. Box #3 items need careful consideration: despite their difficulty, they deserve implementation because of their high impact.[3]

Assigning Priorities

This methodology identifies all the preservation needs of the collections and the actions recommended to meet the needs and then prioritizes the actions for implementation. The needs and actions are provided in your assessment(s) report(s). You may want to ask staff who work with the collections daily to provide additional input on needs and actions. They may be more familiar with less obvious ones than assessors whose time with the collections may be limited. When assigning priorities, first compile a list of all the needs and actions. Then consider the impact and feasibility of each action, and factor in urgency and relevant information from the *Description of Collections*. Based on this combination of information, assign a value of high, medium, or low to each one.

Looking again at the example of rehousing an archival collection that is central to an institution's mission in acid-free folders and boxes, this would be of high impact because the useful life of the collection would be extended significantly and would be readily feasible because the cost of supplies would be relatively low and probably fundable through the budget or donations. High impact and feasibility make the implementation priority high. If instead of rehousing the collection, conservation treatment of each item in it is considered, feasibility would be questionable. The cost would be extremely high, requiring a huge outlay of money. Assuming in-house treatment facilities were not available,

GRID FOR SELECTION OF IMPLEMENTATION PRIORITIES

	High IMPACT Low	
High FEASIBILITY **Low**	**1** Create an emergency response plan Create a building maintenance plan and work with plant operations to implement it	**2** Replace fluorescent lamps in Special Collections with LED lamps
	3 Install a building-wide environmental control system	**4** Redecorate the Special Collections reading room

This grid was developed by Pamela Darling as a tool for comparing the priority of preservation actions in libraries. Actions are ranked high or low in feasibility (likelihood of implementation in a specific institution) and impact (the quantity of material to be affected, the relative value of the material, and the magnitude of the preservation result). They are plotted on the grid. For example, replacing fluorescent lamps with LED ones will reduce fading and photochemical damage on exposed surfaces, but overall deterioration may be reduced more by good climate control. Installing LED lamps is a strategy that administrators understand, will save money long term, and is relatively easy to implement. This is low impact but high feasibility.

Actions that fall in box 1 (high/high) have high priority. Box 4 actions (low/low) can probably be postponed or disregarded. Relative priority of actions falling in boxes 2 and 3 can be determined based on cost, importance in the institutional culture, visibility, and other variables.

Figure 2.1. Grid for Selection of Implementation Priorities.

Adapted by Karen Motylewski, principal; Karen Motylewski, consulting; and updated for this publication by Sherelyn Ogden. Grid reproduced with the kind permission of the Association of Research Libraries from *Preservation Planning Program: an Assisted Self-Study Manual for Libraries*, by Pamela W. Darling with Duane E. Webster, expanded 1987 edition (Washington, DC: Association of Research Libraries, Office of Management Studies, 1987).

this would necessitate obtaining grant funding to contract the services of outside conservators. Staff would need to spend considerable time preparing a grant application and, if successful, additional time preparing materials to be sent to conservators. Unless rehousing were included as part of treatment, this would still need to be done, and the overall impact of this action would be limited. Questionable feasibility and limited impact make the implementation priority medium or low.

If your institution has a lot of actions, prioritizing in two operations rather than one may be easier. This often is the case for institutions that have dozens of needs and actions. Again, begin by compiling a list of all the preservation needs of the collections and the actions recommended to meet them. Then assign a priority of high, medium, or low to each action based on your evaluation of its *importance* in preserving the collections. Rely on your knowledge of the collections and use your judgment to assign this priority—the *institutional* priority. Then determine the *implementation* priority by factoring in the impact, feasibility, and urgency, and considering any relevant information from the *Description of Collections*. When assigning the implementation priorities, begin with the high institutional priorities and then move on to the medium and low ones. This helps filter out the lowest priority actions. Note, though, that sometimes a medium or low institutional priority may become a high implementation priority. An example is the use of bookends to hold books upright on shelves so that they do not lean to the side and become structurally damaged. Purchasing bookends may be a medium or low institutional priority. Purchasing and installing them, however, would be easy to accomplish, making this action highly feasible. Its impact would be high because it would benefit every book in the collection. Thus, the implementation priority may be high. The use of both institutional and implementation priorities is illustrated in this book in the worksheets for the Daniel J. Dial Clock Museum and the Hawaiian Historical Society. If you choose to prioritize in one operation rather than two, simply leave out the column on the worksheets for the institutional priority.

This prioritizing process is not as complicated as it may at first seem. Once you become accustomed to considering the relevant factors, the appropriate priority becomes apparent. Using worksheets facilitates the process.

Worksheets Make It Happen

Worksheets are instrumental in drafting a plan. They help you carry out every step of the planning process. They organize and track information and allow you to see large amounts of it at a glance. They help you lay out content so that it can be easily converted into a narrative for some sections of the plan, and the worksheets themselves serve as other sections. They can even help with related activities. One institution pinned the *Action Plan and Timetable* worksheets to the wall to track progress with implementation. Be creative. Make the worksheets work for you.

Preparing custom worksheets has proven in practice to work better than using standardized ones. Every worksheet in this book was created with a basic software table program. Be sure to have someone on your planning team who can do this. Numerous examples of worksheets are provided here. Feel free to copy them, but do not be bound by them. Adapt them to suit your specific needs. How to do this will be evident as you work through the steps. Keep the worksheets basic; the simpler, the better. Decorative or elaborate ones are not necessary. Be sure to create worksheets with expandable cells or textboxes. This is essential as you will be adding different amounts of information into the various cells.

When recording information, abbreviate or condense your language. Some information needs to be repeated as you proceed through the worksheets, so you want to avoid being overwhelmed by verbiage. You do not need to use complete sentences. Notes are acceptable if the information makes sense and can be put into narrative form where appropriate when the final document is drafted. As in all writing, be as consistent as possible in your use of terms and tenses. Make the worksheets for each step as you proceed rather than make them all at once at the beginning. As you proceed, you will better understand what you need.

Use the Checklist

A checklist of procedures to follow when drafting your plan is provided in figure 2.2. This checklist is intended to demonstrate the planning process further, help you move forward methodically, and enable you to monitor your progress. You may want to copy it and keep it close at hand. Check off the procedures as you complete them.

Now that you are familiar with the process, you are ready to draft the plan.

Notes

1. Pamela W. Darling with Duane E. Webster, *Preservation Planning Program, as Assisted Self-Study Manual for Libraries*, expanded 1987 edition (Washington, DC: Association of Research Libraries, Office of Management Studies, 1987), 29.
2. Ibid.
3. Ibid.

PLANNING PROCEDURES CHECKLIST

___ Read *Six Steps to a Long-Range Preservation Plan.*

___ Obtain administrative sanctioning.

___ Inform staff and begin to build their support.

___ Assign the plan development team and hold an initiation meeting.

___ Appoint a team leader, delegate authority for making decisions, decide who will edit and produce final document, agree on level of detail, and establish a schedule.

___ Gather and review relevant documents.

___ Create and complete worksheets for the *Description of Collections.*

___ Create and complete worksheets for the *Collections Excluded from the Plan* if needed.

___ Create and complete worksheets for the *Needs and Prioritized Actions to Meet Needs.*

___ Create and complete worksheets for the *Long-Range Action Plan and Timetable.*

___ Create and complete worksheets for the *List of Preservation Accomplishments to Date.*

___ Create and complete worksheet for the *Title Page* and draft it.

___ Create and complete worksheet for the *Acknowledgments* and draft it.

___ Create and complete worksheet for the *Executive Summary* and draft it.

___ Create and complete worksheet for the *Introduction* and draft it.

___ Gather documents for the *Appendixes.*

___ Pull all sections of the plan together into the final document.

___ Create and complete worksheet for the *Table of Contents* and draft it and insert in the final document.

___ Establish a schedule for regular updating of the plan.

___ Develop strategies for implementing the plan.

Figure 2.2. Planning Procedures Checklist
created by the author

# Chapter 3

STEP 1 Lay the Groundwork

In this first step of drafting the plan you do preparatory work. You get everything in place and set the tone for the rest of the process. Focusing on detail in this step will help you move smoothly through the following ones.

Administrative Sanctioning and Staff Support

Ideally, the director or board of your institution will initiate the formulation of your plan. Often, however, initiation comes from curatorial or conservation staff. If this is the case, obtaining unequivocal authorization from the director and board is essential. The drafting of a plan takes significant staff time and may cause considerable inconvenience. The regular activities of staff who are working on the plan may be delayed or take longer than usual to accomplish, as well as take time and even money from projects that are more visible. Having authorization for the planning process is crucial if this happens. Additionally important is that staff know that drafting a plan is a valid activity and is sanctioned, if not mandated, by the administration at the highest levels. When seeking approval remember to consider the political culture and organizational structure of your institution and make your request appropriately. Also, board approval should be sought only by the director or with the director's permission. Remember to seek approval from your immediate supervisor as well.

Be aware that administrative approval may not be received right away. No one wants to be viewed in a less than positive light, and acknowledging preservation needs can be construed as making an institution's inadequacies public. All collections, however, suffer deterioration, damage, and loss over time. The administration may need to be assured that establishing, maintaining, and working from an effective preservation plan is vital to cost-effectively reducing the rates at which losses occur and is an essential responsibility of those who are charged with the care of collections in the public trust.

Gaining the support of as many staff members as possible is essential. Obviously, all planning must be supported by the administration if resources are to be allocated for the implementation of recommendations. But equally important is the commitment by non-administrative staff if planning is to be effective. Accomplishments will be greater, and goals will be reached more easily if staff at all levels are committed. This is best accomplished by keeping staff informed of the process from the start and including them in it as much as possible. Explain why the long-range plan is being drafted and how it will benefit them. Actively seek their input, and carefully consider their opinions. As a result, the plan will be a better document, and staff will feel that they have an investment in it. This, in the long run, will greatly facilitate implementation.

Assigning a Team and Establishing a Timetable

Once administrative sanctioning is received, select the plan development team. Staff should be *assigned* to work on the plan, not asked to volunteer, so the task is seen as a job responsibility rather than an outside activity. In a small institution, all staff members and even the entire board may work on it, whereas in a large one only a small percentage of the staff will be involved. The best plans are those that have been developed in collaboration with all staff who are involved with preservation of the collections and, if appropriate, outside consultants.

A team approach usually works best. The team should represent a range of knowledge and skills. Its composition depends on the institution's organizational structure and should include representatives of every department having responsibility for collections care. For example, such departments as facilities maintenance, housekeeping, and security should be part of the team. Seek input from appropriate staff members and volunteers who are not part of the team and incorporate their opinions as appropriate. In addition, include at least one member of the administration to keep them informed of the process. If the institution has an advisory committee invite a representative from that as well as from the board if the administration approves. Finally, recruit someone without extensive preservation knowledge who can ask questions and make suggestions from that perspective. As with any team, a leader must be appointed who is responsible for moving the project forward on schedule, as well as for keeping the necessary communication channels open. Select someone who has the interpersonal skills to deal with diverse personalities and any challenges that may arise. Also important is delegating authority for the decisions that need to be made in drafting the plan. The team leader would be one logical choice for this.

Hold an initiation meeting of the plan development team. Give the team a clear directive at this meeting and establish a timetable. Adequate time for preparation of the plan needs to be scheduled. This is important because if the time allotted is insufficient, the people writing the plan will become frustrated and overwhelmed. Some sections of the plan, such as the *Description of Collections*, may require a lot of time to prepare. The timetable needs to be realistic.

Authorship and Language of the Document

The actual writing of the plan can be done by one person or several. If there are several writers, assign an editor to help ensure consistent language and format. Ideally, the writing is done by the collections staff. There should be, of course, considerable consultation and review with non-collections personnel. Still, the actual writing of the document should be done by one or more individuals who have the best available knowledge and understanding of the collections.

The language of the document is important. The plan should accurately describe preservation needs and recommended actions using comprehensible terminology rather than jargon. Avoid using qualifying adjectives whenever possible, particularly those intended to soften rather than realistically present a situation. Language is important when the plan is used to help secure funds for implementing preservation priorities. For example, if preservation needs do not appear to be serious and pressing, a funding agency will not be as sympathetic to the appeal. An honest, clear, and straightforward approach, using direct language free of jargon, is best.

Plan Length

Every long-range plan is different. Plans vary according to the institution's size and type and the preservation needs' complexity. The team must decide, based on the specific institutional situation, how complex, detailed, and lengthy to make the plan. If having a lengthy one is counterproductive because no one will take the time to read it, write a shorter, less-detailed one. As a rule, a plan should be as short as possible. Detailed technical information is best placed in the appendixes. If, however, your institution contains a variety of collections and has numerous diverse needs, you may find yourself writing a long one. If you fear your plan is too lengthy and you cannot write a shorter one, use different sections for different purposes, submitting only the parts you believe will make the strongest argument for preservation in a particular situation. To do this, however, be sure to arrange the plan so that the various sections can be separated from each other easily and used as separate documents.

Three sections of the plan should always be formatted so that they can be separated from the rest. These sections are the *Executive Summary*, the *Long-Range Action Plan and Timetable*, and the *List of Preservation Accomplishments to Date*. You will have many uses for this information. For example, you may want to circulate these sections of the plan to the administration, board, and staff to inform them of the state of preservation in your institution, or you may find it helpful to include this information in funding requests to substantiate and strengthen your appeal for financial support. Having these sections formatted so they can be separated will also make them easier to update. Institutional situations and priorities change, and these sections especially should be kept current and updated regularly. It may prove useful to format two other key sections so that they can be easily separated as well. These are the *Description of Collections* and the *Summary of Each Collection's Needs and Prioritized Actions to Meet These Needs*.

Gather and Review Existing Documents

Some of the text of your preservation plan probably already exists. Documents such as the following contain information that can be used to draft various sections of the plan.

- Mission statement
- List of goals
- Strategic long-range plan
- Collections policies
- Disaster action plan
- Assessment report(s)
- Grant proposals

Also, check your institution's website pages for additional relevant information. Ask staff and even volunteers as appropriate if they can think of any additional materials that might describe the collections, their needs, and current or past preservation activities. Gather all the materials that you can use. Skim them to familiarize yourself with the information they contain so you know what information you already have when writing the plan. When skimming documents that are not related entirely to preservation, such as the institution's long-range strategic plan, you may want to mark or highlight parts that are directly related to preservation.

Maintain Momentum

Finally, it is important when working on the plan to maintain momentum. Avoid becoming mired in the task and getting stalled at any stage of the process. If you tend to work better with a series of deadlines, refer to the *Planning Procedures Checklist* and add target completion dates to each procedure. If you prefer having a series of intermediate deadlines that culminate in the completion of one procedure, break each procedure into parts. The way to do this will become apparent as you read the following chapters. Remember, always keep moving forward from one step to the next. Do not be overly concerned about making a mistake. The plan is not written in stone and can be changed anytime. If you get to the point where you do not know how to continue, refer to the sample plan in appendix 3. If this does not help you, try incorporating less detail. A general, less detailed plan is better than a half-completed one. You can always go back later and add more detail. Also, do not hesitate to consult with someone who has already produced a long-range plan. Always, if you need help, ask for it.

Chapter 4

STEP 2 Describe the Collections

In Step 2, you begin the actual writing of the plan. You compile and record information that comprises the section titled *Description of Collections*. Writing this section is well worth the time and effort required. The information will help you evaluate and prioritize preservation actions and will provide a frame of reference for decision-making and scheduling. In addition, the information may not be assembled anywhere else, making it useful for many non-preservation purposes. Format it so it can be separated from the rest of the plan.

Much of the information needed for this step is recorded in an inventory of the collections. If, however, you do not have one, do not be discouraged. Although working from an inventory is easier, the information probably already exists elsewhere in materials such as the strategic long-range plan, collections policies, assessment reports, grant proposals, website pages, insurance documents, and institutional histories. When gathering this information, ask staff and volunteers if they can think of any other possible sources.

The information needed for each collection includes:

- the name;
- a description;
- the size (number of items) or the volume (liner feet, cubic feet, cabinets, drawers);
- the value (monetary, intrinsic, cultural, associational, bibliographic), rarity, and provenance;
- the significance to the institution or the reason for preserving the collection;
- the condition;
- the use (kind and amount);
- the length of time the collection should be preserved;
- the form in which the collection should be preserved (original, facsimile, digital);
- any special cultural considerations;
- risk factors of note (materials highly prone to degradation, e.g., ground wood pulp paper, cellulose nitrate film, rubber; possible pesticide contamination, e.g., taxidermy and botanical specimens).

Do not be dismayed if you have only a general sense of your collections and find assembling this information a challenge. This is often the case in smaller institutions. Consult the information you have and do your best. Do not become stalled or overwhelmed. If necessary, make an informed guess and add such qualifiers as *approximately* or *perhaps* or *thought to be* or leave that area on the worksheet blank. If, on the other hand, you have an abundance of information, be selective. The level of detail needs to be adequate to enable you to compare the collections, but do not go into more detail than is needed. Be guided by the level of detail used throughout the plan. Be as accurate as possible and as precise as necessary.

Many institutions, particularly smaller ones, have collections that contain a variety of items. For example, a material culture collection may contain furniture, clocks, and toys, or a fine arts collection may contain paintings, sculpture, and ceramics. If this is the case, you can break down collections like these into subcategories, such as Material Culture (Clocks), or Fine Arts (Paintings). Be as general as practicable to keep the number of descriptions to a minimum.

You may wonder how this information is relevant to prioritizing. Consider a first-edition book on brittle ground wood pulp paper that is valuable for its bibliographic significance and thus must be kept in its original form. Then consider a newspaper on similar paper that is valuable primarily for its informational content and can be digitized or microfilmed. Both the value of and form in which each item needs to be saved are influential in deciding how to preserve them. Items that are used heavily for research purposes have different needs from those that are consulted infrequently. Items of high monetary value raise security issues, while those of special cultural significance may raise issues of use and access.

Worksheets help you record and process the information you gather. Two suggested formats for worksheets are illustrated. Feel free to use one of these or create your own. As mentioned above, these worksheets will become the *Description of Collections* in your final document, so they should be easy to read, neat, and compatible in appearance with the other worksheets you use in the plan.

The worksheets that are illustrated here and throughout the rest of this book are intended to serve as examples. They are for the fictional Daniel J. Dial Clock Museum, a small rural institution. The first suggested format is in figure 4.1. It is a simple list of the information needed for one of the collections, the *Material Culture—Clocks* collection. Figure 4.2 is a completed worksheet in the second suggested format, a table format, for a different collection in the Daniel J. Dial Clock Museum, the *Archives*. The list format is easier, while the table format is more consistent with the worksheets used in later steps. Consult the plan for the Hawaiian Historical Society in appendix 3 for an additional example of a *Description of Collections*.

Even though a plan needs to be comprehensive and, if possible, include all of an institution's collections, a few may be left out. It is important to document these along with the rationale for their exclusion. This way, they will not appear to have been overlooked. Two suggested worksheets for this are provided in figures 4.3 and 4.4, one in a list format and one in a table format.

DESCRIPTION OF COLLECTIONS

NAME OF COLLECTION
Material Culture – Clocks

Description
The collection consists of tall clocks, shelf clocks, and wall clocks.

Size (number of items) and Volume (linear feet, cubic feet, cabinets, drawers)
157 clocks: 60 tall clocks; 47 shelf clocks; 50 wall clocks.

Value (monetary, intrinsic, associational, bibliographic), Rarity, and Provenance
High monetary value. Includes rare and significant examples of early 19th century clocks.

Significance to the Institution / Reason for Preserving Collection
Supports the mission to collect, preserve, and interpret the history and manufacture of clocks. This is a very significant clock collection for its size and scope.

Condition
All clocks are in relatively good condition with complete mechanisms that are capable of running. Some mechanisms are worn and need overhauling before they can be operated; 42 clock mechanisms need treatment, 45 cases need cleaning, and 15 reverse paintings on glass require treatment.

Use (kind and amount)
Exhibit: 100 on permanent display; the rest exhibited temporarily on a rotating basis.
Research: all support research and are available for study.

Length of Time Collection Should Be Preserved
Permanently

Form In Which Collection Should Be Preserved (e.g., original, facsimile, digital)
Original

Special Cultural Considerations
None

Risk Factors of Note
None

Figure 4.1. Description of Collections
created by the author

26 / Chapter 4

DESCRIPTION OF COLLECTIONS
NAME OF COLLECTION: Archives
Description
Administrative, legal, financial, and collection records of the museum that have permanent and enduring value.
Size (number of items) and Volume (linear feet, cubic feet, cabinets, drawers)
150 cubic feet of records 1 flat file cabinet of architectural plans and drawings of the building and property
Value (monetary, intrinsic, associational, bibliographic), Rarity, and Provenance
These records are the original and permanent documents that record the museum's history and development.
Significance to the Institution / Reason for Preserving Collection
These records document the history and development of the museum and have permanent and enduring value.
Condition
The records are in relatively good condition. There is some damage due to the long-term use of paper clips and rubber bands and improper storage methods.

Figure 4.2. Description of Collections – continued on page 27
created by the author

Use (kind and amount)
Periodic use mostly by staff for reference purposes. Very minor use by outside researchers.
Length of Time Collection Should Be Preserved
Permanently
Form in Which Collection Should Be Preserved (e.g., original, facsimile, new format)
Original format, although selected materials, i.e. financial records, may be considered for digitization.
Special Cultural Considerations
None known.

Figure 4.2. Description of Collections
created by the author

DESCRIPTION OF COLLECTIONS

Collections Excluded From Plan

Name of Collection
Three (1915, 1927, 1937) Dial Company delivery trucks. Trucks are located on the property in a covered separate building.

Rationale for Exclusion
Trucks are owned by the museum but are maintained by a separate trust.

Name of Collection
Collection of thirty American Indian objects. The objects are kept in a locked case in the Director's office.

Rationale for Exclusion
The objects were collected by various members of the Dial family over the course of several years and were donated by the family to the museum. The museum board is currently working with American Indian tribes to return the objects to their communities of origin.

Figure 4.3. Description of Collections
created by the author

DESCRIPTION OF COLLECTIONS	
Collections Excluded from Plan	**Rationale for Exclusion**
Three (1915, 1927, 1937) Dial Company delivery trucks. Trucks are located on the property in a covered separate building.	Trucks are owned by the museum but are maintained by a separate trust.
Collection of thirty American Indian objects. The objects are kept in a locked case in the Director's office.	The objects were collected by various members of the Dial family over the course of several years and were donated by the family to the museum. The museum board is currently working with American Indian tribes to return the objects to their communities of origin.

Figure 4.4. Description of Collections
created by the author

Chapter 5

STEP 3 Identify Needs and Actions and Prioritize Them

In this step, you assemble and organize the information you need to generate an action plan and timetable. First you identify your institution's preservation needs and actions. Then you list the resources required for implementation of the actions. Last, you prioritize the actions. You consider the impact and feasibility of each action and factor in urgency and relevant information in the *Description of Collections*. Based on this combination of information you assign a value of high, medium, or low to each one.

Worksheets help you record and organize the information you extract from your assessment(s) report(s). See figure 5.1 for a worksheet in table format that has functioned well in practice and is easy to produce using a software table program. It has columns for identified needs, preservation actions, resources required, and priorities. As many rows as needed can be built into the worksheet and can be added or deleted as required. When making the worksheet, ensure that each cell of the table expands when text is entered to accommodate as much information as needed. The worksheet itself will likely be several pages in length. When completed, this worksheet will be included in the plan to serve as a permanent preservation record. Refer to the worksheet *Summary of Needs and Prioritized Actions to Meet These Needs* in the plan for the Hawaiian Historical Society in appendix 3 to see an example of a completed worksheet.

Listing Needs and Actions

This step identifies the specific actions required to meet preservation needs. For example, the recommended action to meet the need to improve map storage may be purchasing special furniture (e.g., flat storage drawers). The recommended action to meet the need to improve the storage of moccasins may be providing rigid shoe mounts. The recommended action to meet the need for enhanced security may be purchasing and installing new locks on specific doors.

Preservation needs and actions are provided in your assessment(s) report(s). To identify them, you may want to begin by skimming the report(s). Read through a second time, highlighting preservation needs in one color and the recommended actions needed to meet them in a different color. Go through a third time, looking only at the highlighted information, and transfer this information to the worksheets. You may find it useful to note on the worksheets the page in the report(s) where a need or action is discussed in case you want to reread a section of the report(s) later to clarify a thought or to glean additional detail. List each preservation need in the left column and the action

SUMMARY OF NEEDS AND PRIORITIZED ACTIONS TO MEET THESE NEEDS				
Identified Need	Preservation Action	Resources Required	Institutional Priority	Implementation Priority

Figure 5.1. Summary of Needs and Prioritized Actions to Meet These Needs
created by the author

required to meet it in the next column to the right. List every need of which you are aware. Do not discard any because they seem insignificant. Once you have gone through the assessment(s), check other possible sources of information to identify all preservation needs and actions.

Sometimes one need will require several actions, often in sequential order. When multiple actions are required, list the same need repeatedly in the left column and list each different action next to it in the column to the right. An example is the need to enhance fire protection. Actions may include drafting an emergency response plan, installing additional detection devices, and scheduling annual walk-throughs with first responders. Another example is the need to reduce wide fluctuations in temperature and relative humidity. Actions required may include systematically measuring and recording the temperature and relative humidity to determine when the fluctuations occur and how great they are, followed by hiring a consultant to examine the building and its mechanical systems and recommend how best to reduce the fluctuations. This, in turn, would be followed by raising the money to implement the recommendations and then hiring a contractor to carry out the work.

Large, long-term planning projects can be incorporated into the preservation plan the same way. This adds a level of complexity to the plan that may be challenging at first. However, as you become used to the process of breaking large projects into their parts, this will become easier. Consider the need to renovate a large storage space devoted to the storage of a variety of three-dimensional objects. The purpose of the renovation would be to improve conditions and increase capacity. The actions this would require may be hiring an architect to produce a layout with drawings, getting a cost estimate from a contractor to do the work, raising the necessary funds, moving the collections into temporary storage, doing the renovation work, and finally moving the collections into the new space. All these actions can be listed individually and sequentially in the plan next to the same need to renovate the three-dimensional storage space. Integrating large, long-term projects into the preservation plan has several advantages. It helps keep the project on schedule, avoids scheduling conflicts, and reduces the possibility of some actions taking precedence over others.

Listing Needs and Actions Randomly or by Category of Need, Collection, or Institution-Wide

If your preservation needs and actions are limited, listing them on the worksheets(s) randomly works well. You may find it easiest to list them in the order that they appear in the assessment(s). This is the simplest way to proceed and is sufficient for many institutions. See figure 5.2, a completed worksheet with preservation needs listed randomly.

If, however, your institution is large, with many diverse needs and actions, you may find it useful to list them by categories of need. For example, all the needs and actions related to storage can be listed together. Although needs differ for each institution, most fall within the same general categories: environment; storage (facilities, furniture, and containers); exhibitions; conservation treatment; security and access; housekeeping; policies and practices; professional outreach; funding; staff, consultants, and training; reformatting; sustainability; and cultural considerations. These categories are described in figure 5.3. Note that you need not be bound by these categories. If others work better for you, use those.

When needs and actions are numerous, organizing them by category allows you to see at a glance what, for instance, all of the institution's environmental or conservation treatment needs are. This facilitates planning. If you are going to apply for a grant to upgrade the institution's environmental conditions, knowing what all the institution's recommended actions are will help you incorporate as many of them as possible into the application. If you have a donor who prefers to fund the treatment of objects, you can look at this category and see immediately what projects are needed and select one that matches the donor's interests. Figure 5.4 illustrates by category the same needs that are listed randomly in figure 5.2.

Sometimes two categories may be appropriate rather than just one. Citing an example from the worksheet in figure 5.2, severely damaged cased photographs need to be repaired, and funds need to be raised to pay for the conservation treatment. This need could be listed under both conservation treatment and funding. Take care not to get mired down by instances such as this. Be sure to list each need at least once, and listing it more than once is not a problem. If you have several needs that require outside funding, you may instead want to start a separate worksheet that is devoted specifically to this category. This is a good example of creating a custom worksheet to meet your specific needs. The Hawaiian Historical Society chose to do this. Refer to the worksheet "List of Actions and Items Requiring Funding" in the appendix of their plan.

SUMMARY OF NEEDS AND PRIORITIZED ACTIONS TO MEET NEEDS

Identified Need	Preservation Action	Resources Required	Institutional Priority	Implementation Priority
Need additional space for Archives records	Purchase and install additional shelving in Archives storage area	$6,000 outside contractor, outside funding	High	Low
Conservation technician needs training in advanced paper repair	Contract in-house training program in paper repair	$3,000 outside funding, IMLS, staff time to apply for grant	Medium	Medium
Clock cases are dirty and need cleaning	Surface clean clock cases	In-house treatment, conservator	Medium	High
Stack area is dirty, particularly on the tops of the shelving units, and needs cleaning	Implement regular housekeeping schedule for dusting Library stacks	Housekeeping	Medium	High
Books need protection from damage by UV rays emitted from fluorescent lamps in Library	Replace fluorescent lamps in Library with LED lamps	$200 operating budget, maintenance	High	High
Glass plate negatives need protective enclosures and housing in acid-free boxes	Purchase acid-free enclosures and rehouse glass plate negatives	$600 operating budget, conservation technician's time	High	High
Museum needs emergency preparedness plan	Form inter-departmental committee to draft emergency plan	Substantial staff time	High	High
Cases severely damaged on cased photographs and need repair	Apply for outside funding to treat cased photographs	$7,000 outside funding, time of librarian and development	High	High

Figure 5.2. Summary of Needs and Prioritized Actions to Meet These Needs
created by the author

CATEGORIES OF NEED

Organizing the preservation needs of your institution by category may be helpful. Although categories will differ for each institution, most needs fall within the following areas.

Environment Improve environmental conditions for collections; this includes temperature, relative humidity, light, air quality, and pest management.

Storage: Facilities, Furniture, and Containers Improve and/or expand storage facilities and provide for the proper housing and storage of collections.

Exhibitions Address the specialized needs of collections on exhibit.

Conservation Treatment Improve and/or expand collections conservation: analysis, documentation, condition review, treatment.

Security and Access Strengthen systems and procedures for protecting collections from theft, vandalism, fire, natural disasters, and pandemics.

Housekeeping Improve the routine cleaning and handling of collections and storage spaces.

Policies and Practices Develop needed policies and plans and update existing ones. Such policies and plans may include emergency preparedness plan, collections management policy, and long-range preservation plan.

Preservation Outreach Maintain and improve the institution's ability to serve as a preservation resource for the general public and outside professionals.

Funding Raise additional resources to support collections preservation activities while maintaining and expanding existing operational funding.

Staff, Consultants, and Training Maintain and enhance staffing for collections preservation, expand ongoing training for collections staff, and secure resources for outside consultants as needed.

Reformatting Preserve collections by migrating into a different format or updating existing formats.

Sustainability Responsibly incorporate new and developing measures to protect the environment and maintain viability of institutions while still protecting and preserving collections.

Cultural Considerations Address special needs of collections or constituencies to preserve and protect the intangible value of cultural heritage. May touch upon all the areas above.

Figure 5.3. Categories of Need
created by the author

SUMMARY OR NEEDS AND PRIORITIZED ACTIONS TO MEET NEEDS

Identified Need	Preservation Action	Resources Required	Institutional Priority	Implementation Priority
Environment				
Books need protection from damage by UV rays emitted from fluorescent lamps	Replace fluorescent lamps in Library with LED lamps	$200 operating budget, maintenance	High	High
Storage: Facilities, Furniture, and Containers				
Need additional space for Archives records	Purchase and install additional shelving in Archives storage area	$6,000 outside contractor, outside funding	High	Low
Glass plate negatives need protective enclosures and housing in acid-free boxes	Purchase acid-free enclosures and rehouse glass plate negatives	$600 operating budget, conservation technician time	High	High
Staff, Consultants, and Training				
Conservation technician needs training in advanced paper repair	Contract in-house training program in paper repair	$3,000 outside funding, IMLS, staff time to apply for grant	Medium	Medium
Conservation Treatment				
Clock cases are dirty and need cleaning	Surface clean clock cases	In-house treatment, conservator	Medium	High
Cases severely damaged on cased photographs and need repair	Apply for outside funding to treat cased photographs	$7,000 outside funding, time of librarian and development	High	High
Housekeeping				
Stack area is dirty, particularly on the tops of the shelving units, and needs cleaning	Implement regular housekeeping schedule for dusting Library stacks	Housekeeping	Medium	High
Policies and Practices				
Museum needs emergency preparedness plan	Form inter-departmental committee to draft emergency plan	Substantial staff time	High	High

Figure 5.4. Summary of Needs and Prioritized Actions to Meet These Needs
created by the author

You may want to list needs and actions by collection instead. See figure 5.5. This may be the case if some collections are more closely aligned with the institution's mission than others or if certain collections have special funds allocated for their care. If a particular preservation need applies to every collection, it can be listed under the heading *Institution-Wide*. For example, if the institution needs an emergency response plan, list this in the left column and the recommended action to meet this need—form a committee and draft an emergency plan—in the next column to the right. If the institution has an infestation of carpenter ants, list in the left column the need to eradicate the carpenter ant infestation and in the next column the recommended action to hire an exterminator. See the last row of the worksheet in figure 5.5.

Resources Required

In this space on the worksheet, enter the resources required to accomplish each action that is listed. Be as specific as possible, including such information as who is responsible for carrying out each activity, the resources required, and the means for implementation (sources of funding and staffing). This information is useful because it tells staff what they need for implementation so they can plan accordingly. It is also helpful for institutional budgeting, the preparation of grant proposals, and donation requests. You may want to ask board members who are part of the team to assist with determining required resources. They bring a different perspective from that of staff who may already feel overwhelmed by tasks and strained budgets. Also, having board members understand firsthand the costs involved is important.

Assign Priorities

Now you prioritize the actions you have identified. Begin by reviewing the discussion of prioritizing in chapter 2 and take another look at the grid provided there. You assign a value of high, medium, or low to each action and enter it in the worksheet. Note that the worksheet has two columns for priority—institutional and implementation. Whether you need one or both columns is determined by whether you prioritize in one or two operations. If your actions are limited in number, prioritizing in one operation is easier. If, however, you have dozens of actions, doing it in two is easier.

Let's consider doing it in one operation first. Assign a value of high, medium, or low to each action and enter it in the column in the worksheet for *implementation priority*. Base the value on a combination of factors. First, consider the impact and feasibility of each action. Those that have high impact *and* are achievable should be given the value *high*. Those that are of little impact or very difficult to accomplish, or both, probably should be given a value of *low*. The remaining actions may prove more difficult to assign a value, but many can probably be assigned at least *medium* because they have high impact or are easy to implement. Urgency is also a consideration. All other factors being equal, actions that are urgently needed merit a *high* value. Finally, factor in the relevant information from the *Description of Collections*.

Now let's consider prioritizing in two operations. Begin by assigning an *institutional* priority to each action. Assign a priority of high, medium, or low to each action based on your evaluation of its *importance* in preserving the collections. Rely on your knowledge of the collections and use your judgment to assign this priority. Enter the value in

SUMMARY OF NEEDS AND PRIORITIZED ACTIONS TO MEET THESE NEEDS

Identified Need	Preservation Action	Resources Required	Institutional Priority	Implementation Priority
Archives				
Need additional space for Archives records	Purchase and install additional shelving in Archives storage area	$6,000 outside contractor, outside funding	High	Low
Conservation technician needs training in advanced paper repair	Contract in-house training program in paper repair	$3,000 outside funding, IMLS, staff time to apply for grant	Medium	Medium
Research Library				
Books need protection from damage by UV rays emitted from fluorescent lamps in Library	Replace fluorescent lamps in Library with LED lamps	$200 operating budget, maintenance	High	High
Stack area is dirty, particularly on the tops of the shelving units, and needs cleaning	Implement regular schedule for dusting Library stacks	Housekeeping	Medium	High
Visual Materials				
Cases severely damaged on cased photographs and need repair	Apply for outside funding to treat cased photographs	$7,000 outside funding, time of librarian and development	High	High
Glass plate negatives need protective enclosures and housing in acid-free boxes	Purchase acid-free enclosures and rehouse glass plate negatives	$600 operating budget, conservation technician's time	High	High
Material Culture - Clocks				
Clock cases are dirty and need cleaning	Surface clean clock cases	In-house treatment, conservator	Medium	High
Institution-Wide				
Museum needs emergency preparedness plan	Form inter-departmental committee to draft emergency plan	Substantial staff time	High	High

Figure 5.5. Summary of Needs and Prioritized Actions to Meet These Needs
created by the author

STEP 3 **Identify Needs and Actions and Prioritize Them** / 37

the column in the worksheet for *institutional* priority. Then determine the *implementation* priority by factoring in the impact, feasibility, and urgency and considering any relevant information from the *Description of Collections*. When assigning the implementation priorities begin by considering the high institutional priorities first, and then go back to the medium ones, and consider the low ones last. This will provide more context for your decision-making and will help filter out the lowest priority actions. The worksheets for the Daniel J. Dial Clock Museum and the Hawaiian Historical Society illustrate prioritizing in two operations. If you decide to prioritize in one rather than two, simply leave out the column on your worksheet for the institutional priority.

Once you have completed prioritizing, you are ready to schedule implementation of actions and to draft the *Long-Range Action Plan and Timetable*.

Chapter 6

STEP 4 Schedule Actions

In this step, you create the *Long-Range Action Plan and Timetable*, the core of your preservation plan. You do this by plotting on a timetable every implementation priority you identified in the *Summary of Needs and Prioritized Actions to Meet These Needs*. The purpose of this is to ensure that activities are scheduled in a logical order and to specify which activities should begin first and when. The timetable also helps prevent any activities from being ignored or disregarded and keeps implementation on track and moving forward. Plotting the activities is based on the urgency of needs, feasibility, availability of resources, and a realistic assessment of when specific activities can begin and be accomplished. Actions with a sequential or dependent relationship are identified, and the length of time needed to carry out each action is considered.[1] For example, if you need to raise funds for the conservation treatment of a map collection, you may want to list *apply for grant funding for map treatment* one year and *treat maps* one or two years later. Scheduling a low-cost, easy-to-do action early in the timetable may be wise. Interest in the plan will still be keen, and early accomplishments create momentum.

Ideally, the scheduling should be done by staff from across the institution. Careful selection of the people to do this is important. Include someone with institution-wide authority to ensure that the plan is supported and will be carried out. Also, this person should have an overview of all institutional activities and initiatives and be able to recognize scheduling conflicts. In addition, include representatives of collections and conservation. Finally, involve at least a few members of the plan development team to answer any questions that arise about the actions and means of implementation. In a small institution, the board, director, and entire staff may do the scheduling. In a larger one, you may have only one board member, the director, and the staff members who work most closely with the collections. In a large institution, you may have someone with institution-wide knowledge and the authority to report to the director and board as appropriate, along with department heads, conservation staff, exhibits, and development.

A five-year timetable is workable for most institutions, although some large, complex ones may require as much as a ten-year timetable. Use separate worksheets for each year and list the actions that should be carried out that particular year. Once actions are assigned chronologically, their specific order within the year can be considered. If it is convenient and useful, list the actions in priority order, by category of need, or by collection. Otherwise, a random order is satisfactory. You may want to use the order you chose for the *Summary of Needs and Prioritized Actions to Meet These Needs*. List the actions in the left column. In the right column, enter as much information as possible regarding the resources required and the means of implementation. Base this on the information in

LONG–RANGE ACTION PLAN AND TIMETABLE
Fiscal Year 2024 - 2025

Preservation Action	Resources Required / Means of Implementation
Archives	
Rehouse archival records in acid-free folders and boxes	$800, operating budget, librarian.
Install smoke detector.	$100, operating budget, installed by maintenance.
Material Culture	
Purchase floor mats and door mats for gallery and outside building. Increase housekeeping activity.	$80 floor mats, $100 doormats, operating budget, housekeeping.
Form committee to develop plan for collections storage expansion.	Committee: curator, conservator, maintenance.
Apply to IMLS to support outside treatment of reverse paintings on glass.	$15,000, outside funding, IMLS, conservator / development.
Construct / install plastic wall in gallery for shelf clocks on exhibit.	$900, operating budget, outside contractor, curator / conservator.
Construct rigid dividers on shelves for shelf clocks and rearrange if needed.	$600, operating budget, in-house maintenance project.
Construct platform for tall clocks.	$800, operating budget, in-house maintenance project.
Begin to treat clock brass and steel movements, etc.	In-house treatment, conservator.
Research Library	
Implement regular housekeeping for dusting stacks.	Housekeeping.
Establish policies and procedures for handling manuscripts by staff and outside researchers.	Draft policy and procedures, librarian.
Draw shades and fit plywood into windows in stacks.	$200, operating budget, maintenance.
Replace fluorescent lamps with LED lamps.	$200, operating budget, maintenance.
Visual Materials	
Purchase archival enclosures and rehouse glass plate negatives.	$600, operating budget, conservation technician.
Institution-Wide	
Form inter-departmental committee to draft emergency plan and begin work.	Staff time, curator, librarian, conservator, maintenance.

Figure 6.1. Long-Range Action Plan and Timetable Fiscal Year 2024–2025
created by the author

LONG–RANGE ACTION PLAN AND TIMETABLE **Fiscal Year 2025 - 2026**	
Preservation Action	**Resources Required / Means of Implementation**
Material Culture	
Construct fire wall and rearrange storage area as needed.	$5,000, operating budget, outside contractor, maintenance / conservator.
Investigate funding sources and apply to hire a facilities planner to develop collections storage expansion space.	$10,000, outside funding, conservator / curator / development.
Hire specialist to treat reverse paintings on glass.	$15,000, outside funding, IMLS, conservator.
Continue to treat clocks.	In-house treatment, conservator.
Conservator attends training seminar on wood identification.	$1,500, operating budget, conservator.
Archives	
Apply to IMLS to support training for conservation technician in advanced paper repair.	$3,000, outside funding, IMLS, librarian / development.
Visual Materials	
Investigate sources for outside funding to treat cased photographs and submit proposal.	$7,000, outside funding, librarian / development.
Institution-Wide	
Finalize emergency plan.	Inter-departmental committee.

Figure 6.2. Long-Range Action Plan and Timetable Fiscal Year 2025–2026
created by the author

LONG–RANGE ACTION PLAN AND TIMETABLE **Fiscal Year 2026 - 2027**	
Preservation Action	**Resources Required / Means of Implementation**
Material Culture	
Hire facilities planner to develop collections storage expansion plan.	$10,000, outside funding, conservator.
Continue to treat clocks.	In-house treatment, conservator.
Surface clean clock cases.	In-house treatment, conservator.
Archives	
Implement training program for conservation technician in advanced paper repair.	$3,000, outside funding, IMLS.
Visual Materials	
Hire outside conservator to treat cased photographs.	$7,000, outside funding, librarian.
Institution-Wide	
Replace outside perimeter drain.	$7,500, operating budget, outside contractor, maintenance.

*Figure 6.3. Long-Range Action Plan and Timetable Fiscal Year 2026–2027
created by the author

LONG–RANGE ACTION PLAN AND TIMETABLE Fiscal Year 2027 - 2028	
Preservation Action	**Resources Required / Means of Implementation**
Archives	
Investigate outside funding sources for additional shelving and submit proposal.	$6,000, outside funding, librarian / development.
Material Culture	
Acquire additional shelving for clocks.	$800, operating budget, conservator.
Finalize and review plan for collections storage expansion.	Committee reviews and finalizes plan.
Continue to treat clocks.	In-house treatment, conservator.
Research Library	
Purchase and install exhibit cases with exterior lighting for manuscripts.	$2,400, operating budget, librarian / curator.
Institution-Wide	
Install motion-detectors in all areas of the museum and connect to central reporting system.	$2,500, operating budget, outside contractor.

Figure 6.4. Long-Range Action Plan and Timetable Fiscal Year 2027–2028
created by the author

LONG–RANGE ACTION PLAN AND TIMETABLE
Fiscal Year 2028 - 2029

Preservation Action	Resources Required / Means of Implementation
Archives	
Purchase and install additional shelving for archives storage area.	$6,000, outside funding, librarian.
Material Culture	
Begin to investigate funding options for collections storage expansion.	Committee investigates funding options and develops plan.

Figure 6.5. Long-Range Action Plan and Timetable Fiscal Year 2028–2029
created by the author

LONG–RANGE ACTION PLAN AND TIMETABLE
After 2029

Preservation Action
Begin collections storage expansion project.
Create part-time assistant conservator position.
Long-term priority: Create labels with accession number and name for each clock and attach to appropriate shelves in storage.

Figure 6.6. Long-Range Action Plan and Timetable after 2029
created by the author

the *Summary of Needs and Prioritized Actions to Meet These Needs* and on your knowledge of the institution. All actions should be listed. If any actions cannot be included within the timetable period, they should be recorded on a separate worksheet labeled *After* with the date of the last year or labeled *Long-Term Priorities*. This is important to maintain a complete list of preservation needs. See the action plan and timetable for the Daniel J. Dial Clock Museum in figures 6.1–6.6 for guidance.

If an annual breakdown is too specific, actions can be plotted simply as short-, medium-, and long-range. This, however, may prove in practice to be too vague, leaving readers of the plan wondering which actions should be taken first. In this case, you may want to label those actions *begin* or *do first*. Or you may want to match the time frames used in the institution's other planning documents that may be set up on a short-, medium-, or long-range schedule.

This section of the plan should be formatted so that it can be separated from the rest of the plan. This will enable it to be used as a separate tool for planning purposes. Be sure to update this section regularly and move any actions not accomplished in one year to the next so you do not lose track of them.

Note

1. Pamela W. Darling with Duane E. Webster, *Preservation Planning Program, As Assisted Self-Study Manual for Libraries*, expanded 1987 edition (Washington, DC: Association of Research Libraries, Office of Management Studies, 1987), , 110.

Chapter 7

STEP 5 Compile a Record of the Institution's Preservation Accomplishments

In this step, you draft the section of the plan called *List of Preservation Accomplishments to Date*. This is exactly what it appears to be—a list of all the actions related to preservation that the institution has achieved over the years. The section's title can give inclusive dates, such as 2017–2024, or it can be open-ended. Leaving it open-ended makes updating easier. Information in the list can be organized randomly, chronologically, or by category of need, such as environment or conservation treatment. Chronologically is the easiest and is sufficient. You may want to put the most recent accomplishments at the end so that actions can be added easily when the list is updated. See figure 7.1 for a suggested worksheet in table format.

Record every action you can recall and ask long-term staff what actions they can remember. Make the list as complete as possible and go back as many years as you can. If you do not know exactly when an action occurred, add *approximately* or *pre-* before an estimated year, or you can state *date unknown* or simply enter a question mark in the column marked *Year*. When addressing actions repeated yearly, state *ongoing* in the *Year* column.

Do not underestimate what a powerful record this can be. The purpose of this section is to record what has been accomplished and to document progress. This information is useful to include in grant applications and other requests for funding because it shows that the institution can achieve its goals, put its resources to good use, and is a responsible steward of the collections. For this reason, it may be helpful to include funding sources next to the actions if you know them. Seeing the list of achievements also gives staff a sense of accomplishment and pride in their work.

Format this section of the plan so that it can be separated from the rest of the plan and used as a separate document. Also, because you want to keep this section as current as possible, it should be formatted so that information can be added or updated easily. You may want to coordinate its updating with that of the *Long-Range Action Plan and Timetable*. That way, accomplished actions can be moved conveniently from the timetable to this list.

LIST OF PRESERVATION ACCOMPLISHMENTS TO DATE	
Preservation Action	**Year**
The museum has a full-time conservator with a specialization in the care and treatment of clocks. In addition, a part-time conservation technician works in conjunction with the conservator to perform basic treatment of the books and manuscripts in the collections.	Ongoing
Robert Gear, Clock Conservator, conducted an assessment of the clock collection.	2017
Henry Hand, Environmental Engineer, conducted an environmental assessment of all collections storage spaces.	2019
Barbara Band, Book and Paper Conservator, conducted an assessment of the Research Library materials.	2021
Funding was obtained from IMLS to support training of the conservator in specialized clock repair techniques.	2022
Funding was obtained to treat wall maps.	2022
Funding was obtained to conduct an assessment of the visual materials collection.	2023
Funding was obtained from IMLS to help develop a long-range preservation plan.	2023
Francis Face, Photograph Conservator, conducted an assessment of the visual materials collection.	2024
A Long-Range Preservation Plan was produced.	2024

Figure 7.1. List of Preservation Accomplishments to Date
created by the author

Chapter 8

STEP 6 Draft the Introductory Information and Prepare the Final Document

You are almost there. You are about to produce a long-range preservation plan. In this step, you draft the preliminary sections of the plan and pull the document together into one cohesive whole. The preliminary sections include the title page, acknowledgments, executive summary, table of contents, and introduction. Because these sections appear in the front of the plan, you may assume that they are written first. They, however, depend on content developed for the rest of the plan and, for that reason, are written last. Worksheets are included here though you probably will not need them for every section. Use them when helpful and ignore them when not.

Title Page

This page identifies the document. It includes the name of the institution; place or address; the date the plan was completed; the title of the plan; and the name of funding source(s) if applicable. If you wish, you can add a statement of the institution's proprietary rights to the document to ensure that permission is requested before any of the content of the document is copied. If you have no objections to the document being copied and distributed, such a statement is unnecessary. See the worksheet in figure 8.1.

Acknowledgments

This section recognizes the plan development team and everyone else who helped. Include a brief statement regarding each person's contribution. If outside funding was used to support the production of the plan, the funding source should be recognized. You may want to use the worksheet provided in figure 8.2 to assist you in compiling the information you need because this information should be converted into narrative. The *Acknowledgments* is not only a statement of recognition, but also a tool in its own right. It is a way of authorizing the preservation plan. The *Acknowledgments* shows the wide level of involvement of staff, board, and others in formulating the plan. By documenting the individuals and organizations who gave their time and resources to produce it, the *Acknowledgments* demonstrates support for and recognition of the importance of preservation planning.

50 / Chapter 8

TITLE PAGE

Long-Range Preservation Plan

Title of Plan

The Daniel J. Dial Clock Museum

55 Tick Tock Road

Spring Valley, Connecticut

Name and Address of Institution

June 1, 2024

Date

Funded in part by the Institute of Museum and Library Services

Funding Source

Figure 8.1.   Title Page
created by the author

ACKNOWLEDGMENTS		
Authors		
Name	**Position / Institution**	
Susan Second David Dial Martha Minute	Curator of Collections / Daniel J. Dial Clock Museum Conservator / Daniel J. Dial Clock Museum Librarian / Daniel J. Dial Clock Museum	
People Who Provided Assistance		
Name	**Position / Institution**	**Nature of Assistance**
Steven J. Dial	Chairman of Board of Trustees, Chairman of Trustee Collections Committee Daniel J. Dial Clock Museum	Consultation and review of plan
Mark H. Dial	Director / Daniel J. Dial Clock Museum	Consultation and review of plan
James K. Striker	Maintenance Director / Daniel J. Dial Clock Museum	Consultation and review of plan
Outside Sources of Funding Used to Produce Plan		
Name	**Aspect Funded**	
Institute of Museum and Library Services	Support for consultant to conduct a preservation assessment and provide report	

Figure 8.2. Acknowledgments
created by the author

Executive Summary

A summary of the plan, with an action plan and overall time frame, is essential. Its purpose is to acquaint the reader quickly with the institution's preservation plan. It can be

EXECUTIVE SUMMARY		
Essential Points		
Areas of focus: Facilities and storage, environment, conservation treatment, security, exhibitions, policies, housekeeping, staff.		
Highest Priority Issues		
Archives: Rehouse records, improve shelving in storage area, install smoke detector. Material Culture: Improve storage and exhibit procedures, treat clocks and reverse paintings on glass, increase housekeeping activity, obtain wood identification training for conservator, and expand collection storage area. Research Library: Protect collection from exposure to natural light and UV rays, develop policy and procedures for handling manuscripts, improve housekeeping, obtain advanced training for conservation technician. Visual Materials: Treat cased photographs and rehouse glass plate negatives. Institution-Wide: Draft emergency preparedness plan and replace exterior perimeter drain.		
Action Plan and Time Frame		
Implementation Priorities	**When to Begin**	**Resources Required**
Improve environment for Archives and Research Library	2024	Combination of operating and outside funding; staff time
Improve storage conditions for clocks	2024	Operating budget and staff time
Improve exhibition procedures	2024 / 2025	Staff time
Treat appropriate collection materials	2024	Staff time and in-house supplies
Draft emergency preparedness plan	2024	Staff time
Replace exterior perimeter drain	2026	Operating budget and staff time

Figure 8.3. Executive Summary
created by the author

STEP 6 Draft the Introductory Information and Prepare the Final Document / 53

used to inform the administration, governing board, funding sources, and other appropriate parties. The worksheet in figure 8.3 will assist you in selecting and organizing information to include. Like the *Acknowledgments*, this section should be converted into narrative. Without going into unnecessary detail, it should provide a brief overview of the plan stating essential points and emphasizing the highest priority issues. It should be short—no more than one page if possible. The wording should be concise, positive, clear, and direct, and the format should make it easy to comprehend at a glance. Update this section regularly when the rest of the plan is updated, and format it so that it can be separated from the rest of the plan and distributed as an individual document.

Table of Contents

The various sections of the plan should be listed with page numbers. This makes the document easier to use for reference and as a working tool. A worksheet for a table of contents is provided in figure 8.4 if you need it.

TABLE OF CONTENTS

Section of Plan	Page Number
Acknowledgments	1
Executive Summary	3
Introduction	5
Long-Range Action Plan and Timetable	7
List of Preservation Accomplishments to Date	17
Description of Collections	19
Summary of Needs and Prioritized Actions to Meet these Needs	21

Appendixes
   List of Actions Requiring Outside Funding
   List of Projects for Interns
	
	27
	29

Figure 8.4. Table of Contents
created by the author

Introduction

The purpose of the introduction is to present the context in which the preservation plan was developed. Figure 8.5 provides a worksheet for organizing the appropriate

INTRODUCTION
Mission Statement of Institution
The Daniel J. Dial Clock Museum is a nonprofit, educational institution. Its purpose is to collect, document, preserve, and interpret the history and development of the craft of clockmaking, the clock manufacturing industry, and clockmakers in central Connecticut from 1800-1900 and, specifically, the Dial family of clockmakers, their business operation, and personal history from 1785 to the present.
Preservation Mandate
The preservation and care of its collections is a primary responsibility of the Daniel J. Dial Clock Museum that guides trustees and staff in their long-range preservation planning.
Past and Current Preservation Activities
The museum has a full-time conservator who specializes in the care and treatment of clocks and a part-time conservation technician who works in conjunction with the conservator to perform basic paper treatments of the books and manuscripts in the collections. Since 2017, the Museum has worked with outside consultants to evaluate, define, and establish preservation priorities. 2017   Robert Gear, Clock Conservator, conducted an assessment of the clock collection. 2019   Henry Hand, Environmental Engineer, conducted an environmental assessment of all collection spaces. 2021   Barbara Band, Book and Paper Conservator, conducted an assessment of the Research Library materials. 2022   Funding was obtained to support the training of the conservation technician in basic book and paper repair techniques. 2022   Funding was obtained to treat wall maps. 2023   Funding was obtained from IMLS to develop a long-range preservation plan. 2024   Frances Face, photographic conservator, conducted an assessment of the visual materials collection.

Figure 8.5. Introduction
created by the author

information, which should be converted to the narrative in the final document. The introduction should include the institution's mission statement because all policies and strategic plans flow from it. A statement of affirmation of the institution's mandate to take care of its collections is also valuable because it serves as a reminder of this responsibility and validates preservation as a high priority for the institution. Finally, a brief history of the institution's past and present preservation activities should be provided. This information reinforces the institution's ongoing commitment to preservation. The historical perspective is also valuable in helping the reader understand the evolution of the preservation program.

Appendixes

Unlike the other sections discussed in this chapter, the *Appendixes* appear at the back of the book rather than the front. Place in them any documents you created to assist in implementing your plan, such as a list of actions requiring outside funding or a list of projects for interns. Other information relevant to the plan can also be included. Name each document so it can be listed separately in the *Table of Contents* under *Appendixes*. A worksheet is not provided because the documents included in the *Appendixes* can be listed in the worksheet for the *Table of Contents*.

Title Page	narrative or worksheet	
Table of Contents	narrative or worksheet	
Acknowledgments	narrative	
Executive Summary	narrative	format for occasional use as separate document
Introduction	narrative	
Long-Range Action Plan and Timetable	worksheet	format for occasional use as separate document
List of Preservation Accomplishments to Date	worksheet	format for occasional use as separate document
Description of Collections	worksheet	
Summary of Needs and Prioritized Actions to Meet Needs	worksheet	
Appendices	narrative or worksheet	

Figure 8.6. Prepare the Final Document
created by the author

Prepare the Final Document

Now you are ready to combine all the parts into the final document. The order in which the sections are listed in the chart in figure 8.6 has proven to work well in practice, but if you prefer a different one, use that instead. The suggested form in which to present the information—worksheet or narrative—is given for each section. Sections of the plan that should be formatted so they can be easily extracted from the plan for various purposes are also indicated. Various methods of combining the parts into the final document exist. One is to simply *copy and paste* all the sections of the plan together into one cohesive whole. Storing the digital version of the plan in several different locations is wise. Printing it out and producing two or three hard copies for storage in different places is also recommended.

Congratulations. You now have a long-range preservation plan that will serve your institution for years to come. Be proud of your accomplishment. You have made a substantial and valuable contribution to preserving the collections in your care.

Chapter 9

A Few Thoughts on Implementing the Plan

Now that your long-range preservation plan is drafted, you need to address implementation. Losing sight of the new document is easy when you are faced with other pressing needs. Measures need to be taken to ensure that this does not happen. The plan will be of no benefit if it is not implemented. You have worked hard to get this far. Keep going.

Put Someone in Charge

Assign responsibility for moving the plan forward. If the institution has a preservation officer, this can logically fall to that person. If not, another staff member can be charged with the task. This should not be seen as an extracurricular activity but as a regular job responsibility, and the person in charge should be held accountable for it.[1] This person needs to track the plan and keep it on schedule. For example, if a delay occurs in one area, staff must be coordinated so that activities and schedules can be adjusted. If interdepartmental difficulties arise, they must be resolved. This person also needs to make periodic evaluations of goals and accomplishments and, if expectations are not being met, must bring this to the attention of the appropriate individual(s).[2]

The person in charge must be diplomatic and skilled at working with people. The way in which the preservation plan is presented is instrumental in how successfully it is implemented. Presenting the plan from the perspective of those being asked to help accomplish it usually works best. Great care must be taken to avoid appearing disrespectful or critical. After all, suggesting that changes be made or new measures introduced may be interpreted by some to mean that they have been doing things inadequately or incorrectly. Equally important is to avoid making colleagues feel defensive. They may suppose that they are being asked to do an unreasonable amount of extra work. Everyone must be mindful that the plan is a team effort. If colleagues raise concerns, the issues must be addressed immediately, and solutions found collaboratively.

Update Regularly

Updating the preservation plan is crucial for implementation. The plan should be reviewed regularly and updated as needed. Changes usually need to be made for a variety of reasons. Institutional priorities may shift. Staffing and funding levels may be reduced.

Events may occur that modify the sequence in which actions can be implemented or the rate at which they can occur.[3] Emergencies may arise. Opportunities may need to be used to an advantage, or accidents may need to be handled. The plan is a living document, and it will need to evolve as the institution's ability to meet its preservation needs alters over time. Another essential reason to review and update regularly is to record achievements. Often progress seems slow. By updating regularly and adding achieved activities to the *List of Preservation Accomplishments to Date*, progress becomes apparent. Seeing actions move from the *to-do* category to *done* gives staff a strong sense of accomplishment.

An annual review coordinated with the budget process is best for most institutions. Ideally, preservation priorities will become part of the institution's overall priorities and be considered with those when objectives for the institution are determined. This usually happens annually before the institution plans and budgets for the coming year. Another reason for an annual review is that the accomplishments of the previous year can be noted in the annual report. Be sure to document in the plan when each update is made. This keeps you on a regular schedule and helps you measure progress.

Market the Plan

Ultimately implementing the preservation plan means selling it to the administration, board, staff, and even the public. To some extent, this was done when the decision was made to draft the plan. The importance of the collections and their preservation was recognized then. Now, however, *all* the institution's priorities are examined, and choices are made between preservation and the others. This is when preservation becomes a marketing task.

Being a persuasive advocate and making a good case for preservation are essential. Nevertheless, when promoting preservation, always remember to operate within the parameters of your institution's political culture. Act within the context of your specific institutional situation. Know what is viable in your setting.

When advocating for preservation, differentiate between real and potential problems and document the real ones so you can use them to make a forceful argument. Showing that serious problems have already occurred, and damage has resulted lends urgency to your cause. Explain needs clearly and simply. Use consistent language in all your discussions of preservation, regardless of whether they are with the administration, board, staff, or public. This helps demystify preservation by enabling everyone to learn and use the same terminology. This, in turn, leads to discussion of preservation at all levels and brings it into the mainstream of institutional activities and concerns. Use good teaching aids when presenting your case and, when possible and appropriate, use actual objects for demonstrations.

Raise the profile of preservation because this will promote it and help increase support. Offering creative, behind-the-scenes tours is one of the best ways to do this. The more dramatic, the better. Tours enable the administration, board, staff, and public to learn about preservation and see why the institution should commit funds to it. The more they know and understand, the better it is, both immediately and long-term. Give tours at every opportunity. Become known as a resource that the administration, board, and staff can call on at any time for an informative, interesting presentation that will help them promote their position and otherwise perform their job. Working closely with the development department if your institution has one is especially important.

When making a case for preservation to the administration, keep in view the big institutional picture and established institution-wide priorities. Remember that the institution is faced with many competing needs and must consider them all. Recognize the institution's broader issues and the outside forces affecting it and show how preservation priorities can be implemented within these constraints. Illustrate how implementing preservation priorities can assist the institution in achieving its other goals.

Support of the board is an important aid in implementation. Part of the board's fiduciary responsibility to the institution is overseeing how money is distributed. The administration will seek approval of the board in funding large preservation initiatives and will respond to pressure from the board to fund preservation priorities they otherwise may not have. One way to gain board support is to make formal presentations but be sure to get the administration's approval to do this beforehand. Make quarterly and annual reviews of progress, updating the board on results accomplished. Explain why preservation is a priority within the institutional framework and how it coincides with the direction in which the institution is moving. Point out that the collections are assets that can lose financial value if the institution does not preserve them and lose the educational, cultural, and aesthetic value for which they were acquired.

Support of the staff is equally important for implementation. Commit to educating staff in preservation matters. Offer lectures, workshops, and seminars on preservation topics so they can see how it relates to their positions. This promotes implementation by showing them that preservation is not just the preservation staff's responsibility but theirs as well. Preservation is everyone's mandate and a shared goal.

Finally, the support of the public should not be overlooked. Their backing is also valuable and contributes to implementation. The public can help fund special projects and can express their support of preservation priorities to the administration and board. Make a commitment to their preservation education. Provide tours informing them of the institution's preservation activities. Offer workshops and seminars on preservation topics related to their personal collections and provide information on how they can care for their collections.

Like drafting the long-range plan, implementing it usually works better as a team effort. Be passionate in your dealings with the administration, board, staff, and public. Share with them your zeal for the institution and the preservation of its collections. Enthusiasm is infectious. Before you know it, all of you will be working together to preserve the collections.

Notes

1. Darling with Webster, *Preservation Planning Program*, 114.
2. Ibid., 113–14.
3. Ibid., 114, 111.

Appendix 1

Using a Long-Range Preservation Plan

My Personal Experience

Cynthia Engle
Executive Director
Hawaiian Historical Society

Established in 1892, the Hawaiian Historical Society (HHS) has a 132-year history. The only constant in our story is the collections we steward. Staff and volunteers change, the trustees on our board term out, and members come and go. The historical materials, however, remain. They are at the root of our mission to preserve, present, and publish the history of Hawai`i and the Pacific. The Hawaiian Historical Society's commitment to advance the accessibility and visibility of its historical collections and its responsibility to the humanities is what keeps the institution focused and adaptable in an ever-changing environment. All new executive directors of HHS must understand the importance of this commitment and see it as their responsibility. Our long-range preservation plan validates the role and importance of the collections and their preservation and maintains continuity and consistency. Personally, HHS's long-range plan aided me when I became the executive director in 2021 and gave me confidence in my new role as caretaker of the institution's collections.

When I began at HHS it was in the midst of major change due to the retirement of long-term staff, the turnover of newer staff, pandemic closures, and global economic uncertainties. Like many cultural heritage institutions at the time, the way HHS operated seemed obsolete in that moment, and the question of its continued survival hovered over our heads. I was hired to immediately stabilize our operations while strategically planning a way forward. In my role as a new executive director, this became for me a time-sensitive task. The faster I understood HHS and how it functioned in its community, the faster I could mitigate risks and create opportunities for a sustainable future. The long-range plan proved to be one of the main tools I used to rebuild our marketing and outreach efforts, restore our reference services, and reimagine a pathway forward.

The plan provided me with institutional knowledge that was not readily available elsewhere. I learned about the policies, plans, and procedures that guided the care of the collections. I became aware of environmental and security concerns and the actions that were taken to deal with them. I became familiar with modes of access to the collections, patterns of use, and the amount of digital asset management that was in place. Most valuable of all, I learned about our collections—their breadth, depth, size, significance, use, and more. All this knowledge enabled me to advocate for the institution and keep it relevant. During the pandemic we closed, and all our historically renowned in-person programming halted. The information from the plan provided me with the perspective and insight I needed to pivot to other forms of marketing and outreach. I developed a stronger social media presence, reached out to local magazines and newspapers for interviews, and revived our in-house newsletter to our members. The immediate goal was to engage and stay at the forefront of the minds of our members and the community at large. An added benefit was that it resulted in monetary donations that aided in stabilizing operations until we could reopen our doors.

My marketing and outreach efforts also resulted in increased requests for access to our collections once we reopened. The long-range plan helped with this as well. In addition to my role as administrator, I am the librarian and certified archivist for HHS. I therefore assist in the research needs of our patrons. As an information professional I am obliged to provide safe access to historical materials. The long-range preservation plan identified the preservation policies and procedures that were needed to maintain the collections for safe access. In response to this, previous executive directors implemented procedures for regular environmental monitoring, integrated pest management, security, and housekeeping. Inheriting these allowed me to simply restore reference services without any hindrances or concerns for the preservation or safety of the collections.

The long-range plan also provided me with background on our relationship with our landlord and fellow tenant. This helped me develop a collegial relationship with the facility director which has led to open communication and promoted valuable learning opportunities. In fact, the long-range plan generates conversations and encourages buy-in from key personnel, board members and stakeholders in general. This past year I used the plan to propose that the annual budget allocate funds for preservation. The plan documented the need for the funds, and my proposal was endorsed by key individuals whom I was able to educate and inform through earlier conversations. The long-range plan helps with planning for future initiatives as well. The pandemic highlighted a deficiency in the digital resources and remote services that HHS could provide for its community. Building a digital infrastructure and online presence is a strategic vision I am pursuing that will enhance the health of the organization. The long-range plan includes recommendations that support our needed digitization efforts.

The previous directors updated the plan by documenting past and current preservation activities which prevented duplication of effort, helped shape future projects, and influenced the strategic vision. This information helped me write three grants in the last six months that included a preservation component. To date, two have been awarded, and we are confident that the third one will be awarded as well. The plan has not only aided me in securing funding for the collections, but also in knowing what actions to take with these funds. At least 25 percent of the actions recommended in the long-range plan have been implemented, and it is my goal to continue implementing recommendations. Also, I shall continue to document what has been accomplished to inform future executive directors. I am present but a moment in the history of the Hawaiian Historical Society, but the long-range plan ensures the continuation of these moments that uphold our 132-year legacy.

Appendix 2

Background on the Hawaiian Historical Society's Long-Range Preservation Plan

Sherelyn Ogden

The Hawaiian Historical Society's (HHS) long-range plan is based on the methodology in this book. You may notice a few inconsistencies between it and the methodology because the methodology evolved over the years to incorporate lessons learned in writing this and other plans. Nevertheless, the plan serves as a good model. Barbara Dunn, who was the administrative director and librarian of HHS when the plan was drafted, hired me to write it with their input. It has been redacted for security purposes and is published here with the kind permission of HHS.

The Hawaiian Historical Society accomplished an impressive amount in three years of focused preservation planning. In September 2011, the Association of Tribal Archives, Libraries, and Museums and the Western Museums Association collaboratively held a conference in Honolulu. Dunn attended a session titled *Surveying and Assessing Collection Needs*, given by the Balboa Conservation Center. She came away from the session with a sound understanding of a preservation assessment, the need to follow one up with a written long-range plan, and the various ways to accomplish this. I met Dunn at this conference, where I was presenting a session on preventive conservation. Helen Wong Smith, a board member of HHS who was also attending the conference, introduced us, and the three of us discussed what the preservation planning process might entail for HHS.

After the conference, Dunn conveyed to the entire HHS board the importance of having a long-range plan based on organization-wide priorities. With board support she prepared a successful grant proposal to the Conservation Center for Art & Historic Artifacts for a preservation assessment subsidized by the National Endowment for the Humanities. This was conducted in September 2012. In April 2013, she obtained funding from the Samuel N. and Mary Castle Foundation for a consultant to prepare a long-range preservation plan for HHS. I completed this in August 2013.

Many organizations have difficulty moving past the preservation assessment to produce a long-range plan. When I asked Dunn how HHS managed this, she explained that everyone she consulted initially emphasized that the goal of planning is the development of a plan, and that the assessment is the *means* to that end, not the *end* itself. Dunn also advised that granting agencies like to see that organizations have gone through the planning process and have identified their highest priority needs. They want to know that funds will be used responsibly. This motivated her and the HHS board to commit from the start to obtaining a written long-range plan.

When Dunn asked me to draft the plan, I considered how best to go about this. Because of the distance of HHS from where I was based and the resulting travel time and costs involved, I could make only one visit to the site. We worked via e-mail, with

Dunn sending me the preservation assessment and additional relevant documents and me sending her a series of worksheets in various stages of completion for review. We had periodic telephone interviews during which I asked questions and she clarified information. When I had done as much as I could off-site, I traveled to HHS, examined the collections and facilities firsthand, and completed gathering and organizing information. At that point, with my guidance, Dunn prioritized the actions I had listed in the worksheets. Then she and her staff methodically looked at each action, considered its priority and the resources needed to carry it out, and decided when it realistically could be accomplished. Once this was completed, I had all the information I needed to finish the plan. I prepared the action plan and timetable, wrote the introductory information, and pulled the sections of the plan together into one document.

I arrived at HHS on a Monday morning in August 2013, and by Thursday afternoon we sent the completed plan to a printer to be copied and bound. Dunn had scheduled a meeting with the board for that Friday afternoon to discuss our planning methodology and findings. This proved very beneficial. It made the planning process *real* for the board, and because they remembered the meeting, they remained conscious of the process over time. It served to get their immediate buy-in and cement their ongoing support.

When Dunn saw the action plan and timetable she wondered if she would have the time to implement it, but she and the board were committed to pressing forward. In September 2013, Smith, who was then the president of the board, applied to the Atherton Family Foundation for funds to hire a half-time preservation archivist. In January 2014, HHS was awarded $25,000 for each of three years. Nicolita Garces was hired as preservation archivist in May 2014.

Obviously much has changed in the way cultural heritage institutions operate in the years since HHS initiated its preservation planning, but the fundamentals of the planning process remain sound: identify needs → identify actions to meet needs → prioritize actions → schedule actions. Being methodical, persistent, and focused on institution-wide priorities still leads to a successful outcome.

Credit: Some of this information was taken from a presentation given by Sherelyn Ogden and Barbara Dunn at a conference held by the Association of Tribal Archives, Libraries, and Museums in Palm Springs, California, in 2014. Dunn's invaluable contribution is gratefully acknowledged.

Appendix 3

Long-Range Preservation Plan

LONG-RANGE PRESERVATION PLAN

The Hawaiian Historical Society
560 Kawaiahao Street
Honolulu, Hawaii 96813

August 2013

Funded by a grant from
The Samuel N. and Mary Castle Foundation

ACKNOWLEDGMENTS

Barbara E. Dunn, Administrative Director and Librarian, Hawaiian Historical Society, requested that Sherelyn Ogden, of Sherelyn Ogden Preservation Associates, prepare the following long-range preservation plan. The plan is based on information provided in the Preservation Needs Assessment Report prepared by Jessica Silverman, Paper Conservator and Preservation Consultant, Conservation Center for Art & Historic Artifacts. Substantial additional information, including prioritizing and scheduling for the *Action Plan and Timetable,* was provided by the following: Ms. Dunn; Helen Wong Smith, President of the Board of Trustees of the Hawaiian Historical Society; Ipo Santos-Bear, Administrative Assistant, Hawaiian Historical Society; and Judith Kearney, Volunteer Cataloger, Hawaiian Historical Society. The plan was developed in coordination with Glenn Mason, former President of the Board of Trustees of the Hawaiian Historical Society, Helen Wong Smith, and Janet Zisk, Chair of the Preservation Committee of the Board of Trustees.

Preparation of the plan was funded by The Samuel N. and Mary Castle Foundation at the encouragement of Mr. Alfred L. Castle, Executive Director and Treasurer of the Foundation. Additional support was provided by the George Mason Fund of the Hawaii Community Foundation and members of the Hawaiian Historical Society.

EXECUTIVE SUMMARY

The Hawaiian Historical Society is a private, non-profit organization. It was established in 1892 by "...prominent Honolulu citizens dedicated to preserving historical materials relating to Hawai'i and to publishing scholarly research on Hawaiian history."[1] Today the Society's focus also includes the Pacific region and Hawai'i's role within it. The preservation and care of its collections is a primary responsibility of the Society that guides its board and staff in their long-range planning. The purpose of this document is to provide a clear plan based on an integration of all collections' needs and on institutional priorities. It is hoped that this will enable the Society to make the most effective use of limited resources to preserve its invaluable collections.

The Society has accomplished a great deal over the years to preserve the collections, and the board and staff are to be commended for their excellent stewardship. Nevertheless, additional important preservation actions need to be taken. The Society has insufficient space for the size of its collections and is in urgent need of additional space. The assistance of a space planner or other appropriate consultant is needed to rectify this situation. The Society needs to make improvements to the environment in its storage areas in order to extend the useful life of the collections. Temperature, relative humidity, light levels, and air cleanliness are topics that need to be addressed. Enhanced protection from damage caused by fire, water, theft and pests is another pressing concern. Housekeeping practices, which are good given the space limitations, also need to be enhanced, and additional storage enclosures of preservation quality need to be provided. Finally, the society's digital resources, both its collections and institutional records, need to be protected through time.

The highest priority preservation actions for the Society are the following.
- As just mentioned, space is a serious concern. Overcrowded conditions are threatening the safety of collections both in storage and in use. Additionally, the lack of space prevents growth of the collections and also the provision of storage enclosures. The services of a space planner, reconfiguring the existing space and the use of off-site storage are possible solutions.
- Of equal concern is the lack of adequate fire detection and suppression. Given the value of the collections and their unique, irreplaceable content, addressing this issue is of critical importance.
- Although the temperature and relative humidity have been maintained at stable and acceptable levels in the past, rapid fluctuations and high levels have been occurring recently as attempts are made to improve conditions in other parts of the building. This is particularly problematic given the local climate and risk of mold growth. Maintaining stable conditions within acceptable ranges for paper-based materials is essential.
- Protection from theft, insects and water damage needs to be enhanced.
- The accumulation of dust and dirt in storage areas poses a threat to the longevity of the collections. An improvement in air filtration as well as cleaning the air ducts, if feasible, would help with this.
- The Society's ability to access its digital content, both collections and institutional records, and also protect this content from loss is a serious matter that must be addressed. A digitization plan to guide projects in a systematic way and a digital preservation policy to protect these resources long term are needed.
- Policies and procedures need to be developed to provide direction for all of the above. This is essential.

The Society is housed within the Hawaiian Mission Children's Society (HMCS) and shares reading room and storage space with that organization. The collections of the HMCS have many of the same preservation needs as those of the Hawaiian Historical Society. Most of the preservation actions listed in this long-range plan would benefit the collections of both organizations. The collaboration and the development of a strong partnership between these two entities should be explored to most efficiently promote the preservation goals of both.

---

[1] The Hawaiian Historical Society website.

Table of Contents

Please note that page numbers have been changed from the original document to conform with this book.

Acknowledgments	66
Executive Summary	67
Introduction	70
Part I	72
Long-Range Preservation Action Plan and Timetable	72
FY 2013 – 14	72
FY 2014 – 15	76
FY 2015 – 16	80
FY 2016 – 17	83
FY 2017 – 18	85
Long-Term Priorities	88
List of Preservation Accomplishments to Date	89
Part II	91
Description of Collections	91
Summary of Needs and Prioritized Actions to Meet These Needs	108
Appendices	121
List of Actions and Items Requiring Funding	121
List of Actions Requiring Collaboration with the Hawaiian Missions Children's Society	125
List of Possible Projects for Interns from Museum Studies Programs, Library Schools or Other Related Graduate Programs	128

INTRODUCTION

The Hawaiian Historical Society is a private, non-profit organization. It was established in 1892 by "…prominent Honolulu citizens dedicated to preserving historical materials relating to Hawai'i and to publishing scholarly research on Hawaiian history."[2] Today the Society's focus also includes the Pacific region and Hawai'i's role within it.

The preservation and care of its collections is a primary responsibility of the Society that guides its board and staff in their long-range preservation planning. In keeping with this mandate, preservation is stated among the goals of the Society, in the library acquisition policy, and in the reading room rules. Also, a substantial amount of the Administrative Director's time is allocated to preservation in that position's job description.

Brief Preservation History

For decades the Society has worked with outside consultants to evaluate, define and establish preservation priorities. As early as 1974 Mary Lee, Paper Conservator at the now defunct Pacific Regional Conservation Center, conducted a survey to determine the preservation needs and priorities of the collections. Between 1982 and 1988, the Society raised $56,500 in grant funds for conservation work. Over the years staff have attended conferences and taken preservation workshops to expand their knowledge of preservation issues. Recently, the Librarian took a workshop on preservation planning. This enabled her to convey to the board the importance of having a plan based on priorities and also to clarify for them the planning process. In 2010 a preservation committee was formed to make preservation recommendations to the board. This resulted in the preparation in 2012 of a successful grant proposal to the Conservation Center for Art & Historic Artifacts for a needs assessment survey subsidized by the National Endowment for the Humanities. The survey was completed early in 2013 by Jessica Silverman, Paper Conservator and Preservation Consultant at the Center. In April 2013, funding was obtained from the The Samuel N. and Mary Castle Foundation for consultant Sherelyn Ogden, of Sherelyn Ogden Preservation Associates, to prepare a long-range preservation plan for the Society.

Purpose of Preservation Plan

The purpose of the plan is to enable the Society to make the best use of its resources by following a path based on achievable needs and institutional priorities. The plan serves as a road map in carrying out preservation actions and in keeping preservation activities on track. Also, it serves as a tool in fundraising, illustrating that resources are being used in a responsible way to meet highest priority needs. If the plan is updated regularly, it will document progress and remain current.

The plan does not include all the institution's preservation needs. Instead, it represents only the most pressing ones---those that must be addressed first. These were identified by staff and in the report of the preservation needs assessment conducted by Jessica Silverman. The needs were then prioritized by staff and board members according to institutional priorities and mission. Once these needs are met, additional preservation needs will be identified, prioritized and met.

Plan Exclusions

---

[2] The Hawaiian Historical Society website.

Three groups of collections materials are excluded from this plan. Books that are accessioned but not cataloged are excluded because they are strictly an access issue rather than a preservation one at this time. The same is the case for gift books waiting to be processed. Duplicates are also excluded because they will eventually be removed from the collections.

Plan Organization

The plan is divided into sections that are listed in the *Table of Contents*. Each section of the plan is intended to stand alone so that it can be separated from the rest of the plan and used for other purposes, such as grant applications. The plan contains a substantial amount of detailed information. Where possible, tables and lists are employed to make this information easily and quickly comprehendible.

Part I lays out what the institution intends to do and what it already has accomplished. The *Long-Range Preservation Action Plan and Timetable* defines the institution's preservation future. It lists the actions required to preserve the collections, indicates which actions are the most important to take first, and schedules these in the most effective way for implementation. It should be noted that the timetable is not unalterable. It may change accordingly as opportunities and obstacles present themselves. Actions may shift from year to year in response to circumstances that arise. The *List of Preservation Accomplishments to Date* illustrates what has been accomplished on a regular basis and documents progress.

Part II and the *Appendices* of the plan provide much of the detailed information required by staff to schedule and implement the preservation actions listed in *Part I*. It provides detailed information about collections, the recommended actions, and the resources required to carry out the actions.

Finally

This is a working document that will change to meet evolving needs of the Society. Comments and suggestions are invited to make this tool as useful as possible for everyone.

PART I

LONG-RANGE PRESERVATION ACTION PLAN AND TIMETABLE

Fiscal Year 2013 - 14

Preservation Action	Resources Required / Means of Implementation
Environment	
Assign responsibility for regular monitoring of temperature and relative humidity and for recording readings	Staff time
Work with HMCS to adjust environmental systems to mitigate temperature and relative humidity fluctuations in vault and improve conditions in general as much as possible.	Staff time initially; may need to bring in consultants and purchase equipment
Work with HMCS to add UV-filtering sleeves to all fluorescent tubes that do not have them	Staff time and funds for additional sleeves
Work with HMCS to reduce levels of visible light in reading room by installing blinds or tinted films on windows OR Reducing bulb wattage in overhead fixtures Or Turning specific rows of lights off when not in use	Staff time and funds for blinds, films or new bulbs
Storage: Facilities and Containers	
Deal with excess copies of books to obtain more space	Funds to hire an appraiser to assess value, set price and arrange for appropriate disposal of excess books
Hire a space planner or other appropriate consultant to help reconfigure space with the goal of obtaining more space	Funds to hire space planner

Preservation Action	Resources Required / Means of Implementation
Locate adequate off-site storage and move appropriate collections there to obtain more space	Staff time, off-site storage space and boxes for storage of books
In collaboration with HMCS, consider transferring HHS collections that are duplicated in the HMCS library to off-site storage and add a note to the catalog record that the item is in storage and the HMCS copy should be used, to obtain more space	Staff time, off-site storage space and boxes for storage of books
If shelving in processing area in vault is not moved during space reconfiguration, stabilize it by bracing with cross bars and fix to walls with strapping	Funds to hire contractor to do this and for necessary supplies
Purchase rolling carts for materials that are currently on the floor awaiting processing	Funds for carts
Hire an electrician to install electric outlets on tables or, at the very least, cover cords with ramp-covers to remove tripping hazard posed by computer cords and power strips	Funds to hire an electrician and/or supplies
Exhibitions	
Protect Clint watercolor from light damage by making a facsimile for display, or limiting light exposure by covering with light-blocking cloth	Staff time and funds for facsimile or cloth
Protect Marshall Islands stick charts from light and other damage by removing them from permanent display if at all possible. If not possible, put in vitrines to protect them from accidental damage, pests and dust, and cover vitrines with light-blocking cloth.	Staff time and funds for vitrines and cloth
Security and Access	
Discuss with HMCS the possibility of installing adequate fire detection and suppression	Staff and board time initially
Ensure that HHS meets local fire codes for safety by scheduling a walk-through with local fire marshal; consult with marshal about outdoor grill and cellulose nitrate film	Staff time and funds for upgrades to meet code

Preservation Action	Resources Required / Means of Implementation
Ensure that local fire department is prepared to respond to an emergency by providing reliable individuals with floor plans marked with salvage priority locations to keep off-site	Staff time
Ensure access to materials by replacing faulty call number labels with ones that have better adhesives. Investigate what other institutions do and implement a new system	Staff time and funds for new supplies
Improve researchers' access to fragile materials by obtaining a drop-edge copier or scanner	Staff time and funding for the copier or scanner
Ongoing – Carried out every year	
Purchase sticky traps for integrated pest management	Staff time and funds for traps
Thoroughly examine all incoming items, particularly collections, for pests	Staff time
Allow only flowers and plants from professional florists to come in close proximity to collections and continue to restrict potted plants	Staff time
Measure UV light levels to ensure that filters are still effective and record date and findings for future reference	Staff time and possibly funds for a light meter if one cannot be borrowed
Ensure access to collections by continuing to process, catalog, and inventory them	Staff time
Remove food trash from offices on a daily basis	Facilities staff time
Ensure stable on-going funding for conservation by maintaining a line item in the budget for conservation	Board and staff time
Identify appropriate grants, match projects to them, and maintain a long-term schedule of regular applications for funding	Staff and board time
Seek donor assistance for special projects or items	Staff and board time

Preservation Action	Resources Required / Means of Implementation
Contact appropriate programs (e.g., museum studies programs, library schools, related graduate programs) in local colleges and universities to find student interns for assistance	Staff time
Obtain on-going hands-on training for staff and board members in emergency salvage techniques and response procedures, Red Cross safety classes, the Incident Command System, and other emergency-related topics.	Staff and board time and funding for training

LONG-RANGE PRESERVATION ACTION PLAN AND TIMETABLE

Fiscal Year 2014 - 15

Preservation Action	Resources Required / Means of Implementation
Environment	
Allocate a space for a quarantine room for incoming materials to protect collections from pests	Staff time and space
Work with HMCS to add weather stripping to front entrance and to caulk and seal all other outside doors	Funds for stripping, caulking and installation
Work with HMCS to develop a regular schedule for changing filters in HVAC system	Staff time and funds for filters
Work with HMCS and HVAC contractor to clean air ducts and improve air filtration by all practical means possible (HEPA air cleaner)	Staff time and funds to hire a contractor and purchase equipment or supplies
Storage: Facilities and Containers	
Implement recommendations of space planner	Staff time and funds for alterations to space
Digitize and transfer all or some of newspaper clipping file to off-site storage to obtain more space	Staff time, off-site storage space and boxes for storage
Allocate a space for processing collections and for the storage of supplies that is separate from collections storage	Funds to hire a space planner or other appropriate person
Facilitate safe retrieval of materials on high shelves in vault by purchasing a proper ladder	Funds for ladder
Begin rehousing items that need this by prioritizing rehousing projects and identifying needed supplies	Staff time and funds for supplies
Prevent books in vault from slumping on shelves by purchasing more bookends for stacks	Staff time and funds for bookends

Preservation Action	Resources Required / Means of Implementation
Conservation Treatment	
Obtain conservation assessment, treatment proposal and cost estimate for Clint watercolor	Funds to pay conservator
Obtain conservation assessment, treatment proposal and cost estimate for Kahanamoku painting	Funds to pay conservator
Obtain conservation assessment, treatment proposal and cost estimate for the Webber engraved atlases	Funds to pay conservator
Security and Access	
Protect digital information from loss by backing up critical electronic records to off-site servers or off-site external hard-drives	Funds for off-site electronic storage and staff time
Develop a system to ensure that back-ups are made at regular intervals	Staff time
Protect collections from water damage by raising them at least four inches off the floor when shifting them after removal of excess books and implementation of recommendations of space planner	Staff time, space and labor to move collections
Store copies of cataloging records and inventories off-site	Staff time and funds to create microfilm copies for off-site storage
Check inventories of collections to ensure that no items are missing	Staff time
Facilitate safe use of books in the reading room by obtaining book cradles and other types of supports that are made of inert materials	Staff time and funding for supports
Housekeeping	
Clean shelves and dust books when shifting collections after removal of excess books and implementation of recommendations of space planner	Staff time and cleaning supplies

Preservation Action	Resources Required / Means of Implementation
Institute a cleaning schedule moving forward	Staff time
Policies, Plans and Procedures	
Set a date for annual review and updating of the long-range preservation plan and adhere to it (e.g., beginning of fiscal year)	Staff time
Expand and complete the emergency plan, adding salvage instructions, updated vendors and contact lists, shelter-in-place instructions, and forms for reporting incidents and inventory control. Gather information, obtain models from other institutions and complete plan.	Staff time to draft additional information
Develop a stricter acquisitions policy that is highly selective	Staff time to draft policy
Develop a digitization plan to guide projects in a systematic way	Funds to hire a consultant and staff time
Ongoing – Carried out every year	
Update long-range preservation plan	Staff time
Purchase sticky traps for integrated pest management	Staff time and funds for traps
Thoroughly examine all incoming items, particularly collections, for pests	Staff time
Allow only flowers and plants from professional florists to come in close proximity to collections and continue to restrict potted plants	Staff time
Measure UV light levels to ensure that filters are still effective and record date and findings for future reference	Staff time and possibly funds for a light meter if one cannot be borrowed
Ensure access to collections by continuing to process, catalog, and inventory them	Staff time
Remove food trash from offices on a daily basis	Facilities staff time
Ensure stable on-going funding for conservation by maintaining a line item in the budget for conservation	Board and staff time

Preservation Action	Resources Required / Means of Implementation
Identify appropriate grants, match projects to them, and maintain a long-term schedule of regular applications for funding	Staff and board time
Seek donor assistance for special projects or items	Staff and board time
Contact appropriate programs (e.g., museum studies programs, library schools, related graduate programs) in local colleges and universities to find student interns for assistance	Staff time
Obtain on-going hands-on training for staff and board members in emergency salvage techniques and response procedures, Red Cross safety classes, the Incident Command System, and other emergency-related topics.	Staff and board time and funding for training
Begin work with conservators to methodically plan for conservation treatment of collections in need of repair and to provide conservation assessments and cost estimates	Staff time and funding to hire conservators

LONG-RANGE PRESERVATION ACTION PLAN AND TIMETABLE

Fiscal Year 2015 - 16

Preservation Action	Resources Required / Means of Implementation
Storage: Facilities and Containers	
Acquire more flat paper storage drawers for maps and similarly-sized items	Funds to purchase drawers and space for drawers
Conservation Treatment	
Contract treatment of Clint watercolor, Kahanamoku painting and/or Webber engraved atlases	Funds to pay conservator
Security and Access	
Work with HMCS to gather salvage supplies into a marked waterproof container designated for emergency use	Staff time and funds for supplies
Protect digital information from loss and inaccessibility by exploring options for digital asset management systems. See also *Policies, Plans and Procedures* for FY2015-16	Staff time initially
Policies, Plans and Procedures	
Set a date for annual review and update of emergency plan and adhere to it (e.g., beginning of fiscal year).	Staff time
Develop a digital preservation policy for protection of digital resources through time	Staff time and funds to hire a consultant
Ongoing – Carried out every year	
Update long-range preservation plan	Staff time
Update emergency plan	Staff time

Preservation Action	Resources Required / Means of Implementation
Continue rehousing items that need this	Staff time and funds for supplies
Purchase sticky traps for integrated pest management	Staff time and funds for traps
Thoroughly examine all incoming items, particularly collections, for pests	Staff time
Allow only flowers and plants from professional florists to come in close proximity to collections and continue to restrict potted plants	Staff time
Measure UV light levels to ensure that filters are still effective and record date and findings for future reference	Staff time and possibly funds for a light meter if one cannot be borrowed
Ensure access to collections by continuing to process, catalog, and inventory them	Staff time
Remove food trash from offices on a daily basis	Facilities staff time
Ensure stable on-going funding for conservation by maintaining a line item in the budget for conservation	Board and staff time
Identify appropriate grants, match projects to them, and maintain a long-term schedule of regular applications for funding	Staff and board time
Seek donor assistance for special projects or items	Staff and board time
Contact appropriate programs (e.g., museum studies programs, library schools, related graduate programs) in local colleges and universities to find student interns for assistance	Staff time
Obtain on-going hands-on training for staff and board members in emergency salvage techniques and response procedures, Red Cross safety classes, the Incident Command System, and other emergency-related topics.	Staff and board time and funding for training
Work with conservators to methodically plan for conservation treatment of collections in need of	Staff time and funding to hire conservators

Preservation Action	Resources Required / Means of Implementation
repair and to provide conservation assessments and cost estimates	

LONG-RANGE PRESERVATION ACTION PLAN AND TIMETABLE

Fiscal Year 2016 - 17

Preservation Action	Resources Required / Means of Implementation
Conservation Treatment	
Contract treatment of Clint watercolor, Kahanamoku painting and/or Webber engraved atlases	Funds to pay conservator
Security and Access	
Protect cellulose nitrate and cellulose acetate from loss by deciding on a plan of action and implementing it	Staff time and perhaps funding depending on action chosen
Consider re-duplicating the nitrate film that has questionable duplicates and disposing of the nitrate through a hazardous waste company or agency	Staff time and funding for duplication and disposal
Policies, Plans and Procedures	
Develop an integrated pest management policy	Staff time to draft policy
Draft a loan policy that includes environmental requirements	Staff and board time to draft policy
Ongoing	
Update long-range preservation plan	Staff time
Update emergency plan	Staff time
Continue rehousing items that need this	Staff time and funds for supplies
Purchase sticky traps for integrated pest management	Staff time and funds for traps
Thoroughly examine all incoming items, particularly collections, for pests	Staff time

Preservation Action	Resources Required / Means of Implementation
Allow only flowers and plants from professional florists to come in close proximity to collections and continue to restrict potted plants	Staff time
Measure UV light levels to ensure that filters are still effective and record date and findings for future reference	Staff time and possibly funds for a light meter if one cannot be borrowed
Ensure access to collections by continuing to process, catalog, and inventory them	Staff time
Remove food trash from offices on a daily basis	Facilities staff time
Ensure stable on-going funding for conservation by maintaining a line item in the budget for conservation	Board and staff time
Identify appropriate grants, match projects to them, and maintain a long-term schedule of regular applications for funding	Staff and board time
Seek donor assistance for special projects	Staff and board time
Contact appropriate programs (e.g., museum studies programs, library schools, related graduate programs) in local colleges and universities to find student interns for assistance	Staff time
Obtain on-going hands-on training for staff and board members in emergency salvage techniques and response procedures, Red Cross safety classes, the Incident Command System, and other emergency-related topics.	Staff and board time and funding for training
Work with conservators to methodically plan for conservation treatment of collections in need of repair and to provide conservation assessments and cost estimates	Staff time and funding to hire conservators

LONG-RANGE PRESERVATION ACTION PLAN AND TIMETABLE

Fiscal Year 2017 - 18

Preservation Action	Resources Required / Means of Implementation
Storage: Facilities and Containers	
Work with HMCS to implement a regular schedule of facilities maintenance	Staff time
Work with HMCS to develop a system to document and compile records of all maintenance projects and assign someone to maintain this record	Staff time
Conservation Treatment	
Contract treatment of Clint watercolor, Kahanamoku painting and/or Webber engraved atlases	Funds to pay conservator
Security and Access	
Expand on-line catalog to include cataloged books	Staff time
Housekeeping	
Formalize all housekeeping procedures; write out procedures, evaluate and specify cleaning products, train staff in desired cleaning practices, establish a regular schedule, and record everything that is done and when it is done. See also *Policies, Plans and Procedures* for FY 2017-18	Staff time
Policies, Plans and Procedures	
Draft an institutional long-range strategic plan. Perhaps develop the outline from the January 2012 meeting into a formal plan.	Board and staff time
Draft a housekeeping manual	Staff time

Preservation Action	Resources Required / Means of Implementation
Develop a collection management policy	Staff time
Ongoing	
Update long-range preservation plan	Staff time
Update emergency plan	Staff time
Continue rehousing items that need this	Staff time and funds for supplies
Purchase sticky traps for integrated pest management	Staff time and funds for traps
Thoroughly examine all incoming items, particularly collections, for pests	Staff time
Allow only flowers and plants from professional florists to come in close proximity to collections and continue to restrict potted plants	Staff time
Measure UV light levels to ensure that filters are still effective and record date and findings for future reference	Staff time and possibly funds for a light meter if one cannot be borrowed
Ensure access to collections by continuing to process, catalog, and inventory them	Staff time
Remove food trash from offices on a daily basis	Facilities staff time
Ensure stable on-going funding for conservation by maintaining a line item in the budget for conservation	Board and staff time
Identify appropriate grants, match projects to them, and maintain a long-term schedule of regular applications for funding	Staff and board time
Seek donor assistance for special projects	Staff and board time
Contact appropriate programs (e.g., museum studies programs, library schools, related graduate programs) in local colleges and universities to find student interns for assistance	Staff time
Obtain on-going hands-on training for staff and board members in emergency salvage techniques and response procedures, Red Cross safety	Staff and board time and funding for training

Preservation Action	Resources Required / Means of Implementation
classes, the Incident Command System, and other emergency-related topics.	
Work with conservators to methodically plan for conservation treatment of collections in need of repair and to provide conservation assessments and cost estimates	Staff time and funding to hire conservators

LONG-RANGE PRESERVATION ACTION PLAN AND TIMETABLE

Long-Term Priorities

Preservation Action	Resources Required / Means of Implementation
Storage: Facilities and Containers	
Consider transferring photographs in file cabinet drawers to Hollinger boxes on shelves with other photographs	Staff time, space on shelves, and funding for boxes
Security and Access	
Catalog backlog of books	Staff time
Protect assets financially by investigating the possibility of an insurance plan or self-insured endowment for collections	Staff and board time and funds for insurance/endowment
Consider digitizing all or part of books in collection of Early Voyages to Hawaii and the Pacific for online research use	Staff time and funding
Improve access to the collection of *Newspapers Published in Hawaii* by exploring new technology to identify a method to produce readable microfilm and digital copies of the originals	Staff time and funding
Improve access to the manuscript collections by digitizing selected collections, i.e. the Stephen Reynolds journal	Staff time and funding

LIST OF PRESERVATION ACCOMPLISHMENTS TO DATE

Purchased archival supplies. Line item in budget, "Library supplies."	Ongoing
Mounted on website the database for historical photograph collection, with selected photographs. Started 2010.	Ongoing
Mounted on website the library OPAC catalog of manuscripts in HHS library. Started 2010.	Ongoing
Received grant from Samuel N. and Mary Castle Foundation to have a Long Range Preservation Plan prepared for HHS. Sherelyn Ogden Preservation Associates prepared the plan. Site visit in July.	2013
Partnered with Adam Matthew Digital in U.K. to have selected books, manuscripts, newspapers, illustrations, and maps in HHS library digitized as part of a China Trade digital collection.	2013
Partnered with Portuguese-American Archives at Univ. of Mass. Dartmouth to have original copies of HHS collection of Portuguese language newspapers digitized and hosted on internet.	2013
Conservation Center for Art & Historic Artifacts (CCAHA) prepared a Preservation Needs Assessment Report for HHS. Grant from CCAHA. Site visit Sept. 2012.	2012 - 2013
Digitized microfilm of Portuguese language newspaper collection and posted it on internet for research use.	2012 - 2013
Received Challenge Grant from Mason Fund for preservation activities.	2012
HHS president appointed Preservation Committee as a standing committee of the board. Tasked with assessing collections and recommending preservation needs.	2010
Purchased Hobo humidity and temperature monitor to replace old monitor.	2009
Librarian attended webinar on security in the reading room.	2008
Upgraded computer system with grant from Atherton Family Foundation.	1999 - 2000
Purchased from Hamburg Museum of Folk Arts prints of 237 glass plate negatives taken by Eduard Arning in Hawaii 1893 – 1896. Copy negs and copy prints made. Housed in archival albums. Prepared finding aid. Grant from Univ.	1997

of Hawaii Committee for the Preservation and Study of Hawaiian Language, Art, and Culture.	
Purchased microfilm reader/printer to replace old reader. Grant from Gannett Community Fund.	1992
Hired a preservation librarian to upgrade storage and rehouse photograph collection, photo albums and negative collections and to set up database finding aid for general historical photograph collection. Grants from State Foundation on Culture and the Arts.	1989 - 1992
Hired a cataloger to catalog backlog of accessioned books for the library. Grants from Samuel N. and Mary Castle Foundation and Cooke Foundation.	1989 - 1990
Microfilmed newspapers in the library collection as part of the U.S. Newspaper Microfilm Project. Grant from State Foundation on Culture and the Arts.	1987 - 1989
Computer system purchased with grants from IBM, Samuel N. and Mary Castle Foundation, McInerny Foundation, and Atherton Family Foundation.	1986 - 1987
Librarian attended AASLH Seminar for Historical Administrators at Williamsburg, VA. Grant from board member.	1986
George Brown manuscript collection (1843 – 1846) purchased. Letters and documents housed in acid free folders. Some letters transcribed and published in The Hawaiian Journal of History. 1985.	1985
Library stack room renovated. Compact shelving installed, new light fixtures installed with ultraviolet filters on lights. New map case, microfilm cabinet, and new file cabinets purchased. Newspaper shelving (warehouse shelves) was reorganized with more shelves installed. 1983 – 1985.	1983 - 1985
Library conservation grants from Hawaii State Foundation on Culture and the Arts and the Cooke Foundation. Five paintings in HHS collection were restored by restoration expert. One ink and wash watercolor was conserved.	1982 - 1987
Librarian attended seminar for American librarians at Oxford University. Grant from board members.	1981
Preserved Theodore Kelsey photograph collection of 500 nitrate negatives. Printed negatives, housed them in archival albums, prepared finding aid, had nitrate negatives duplicated on safety film, nitrate negs and duplicate negs housed in acid free sleeves in archival boxes.	1974 - 1978

PART II

DESCRIPTION OF COLLECTIONS

NAME OF COLLECTION
Early Voyages to Hawaii and the Pacific: published narratives and atlases on compact shelves, oversize shelves, and newspaper shelves.

Description
Historical narratives dating from the late eighteenth and nineteenth centuries. Many of these narratives include illustrations of people and places, natural history, and maps of the Pacific. Several are in languages other than English. A published bibliography of these narratives is based on the libraries of the Hawaiian Mission Children's Society and the Hawaiian Historical Society: *Voyages to Hawaii Before 1860* by Bernice Judd, enlarged and edited by Helen Y. Lind, University Press of Hawaii, 1974.

Size (number of items) and Volume (linear feet, cubic feet, cabinets, drawers)
Compact shelves = 160 linear feet. Oversize shelves = 6 linear feet. Newspaper shelves = 5 shelves plus 2 linear feet.

Value (monetary, intrinsic, associational, bibliographic), Rarity, and Provenance
All of the books in this collection are out of print.

Significance to the Institution / Reason for Preserving Collection
Many of these volumes are the earliest accessions into the library—donated by Society founders. They are included in a published bibliography, "Voyages to Hawaii before 1860," and in the "Hawaii National Bibliography."

Condition
Varies from moderate shelf wear to detached covers. The large folio volumes that go with published narratives of voyages to Hawaii and the Pacific lie flat on the warehouse/newspaper shelves. A few have been restored. Some are in poor condition, for example the 2 copies of the Webber atlas for the third Cook voyage. Most are okay. The shelf space for these volumes is used up. The atlases are stacked 3 or 4 high.

Archival needs
Some atlases need restoration work and/or housing in custom boxes. The use of custom boxes takes up more space and will require more oversize warehouse shelving.

Access needs
All of these large folio volumes are cataloged. For the future it would be useful to digitize these important engravings, lithographs, and maps. Some of the HHS scientific atlases were loaned to the Bishop Museum library on long-term loan some years ago. These are now cataloged in the Bishop Museum collection.

Use (kind and amount)
Both narratives and atlases are used regularly by researchers. These are primary source materials. HHS is known for this collection.

For how long should collection be preserved?
In perpetuity.

In what form should collection be preserved (e.g., original, facsimile, new format)?
Would be a great resource if collection could be digitized for online research use.

NAME OF COLLECTION
Hawaiian-Language Books

Description
Hawaiian texts from mission and government presses dating from 1823. This collection includes hymnals, religious tracts, and school texts translated into Hawaiian and printed by the missionaries for use in teaching the Hawaiian people. There are also a small number of texts in other Pacific languages. A published bibliography includes the holdings of the Hawaiian Historical Society as well as thirty-five other libraries and collections: *Hawaiian Language Imprints, 1822–1899, A Bibliography,* compiled by B. Judd, J. Bell, and C. Murdoch, Hawaiian Mission Children's Society and University Press of Hawaii, 1978.
(Includes some texts in other Polynesian/Micronesian languages)

Size (number of items) and Volume (linear feet, cubic feet, cabinets, drawers)
Location: compact shelves. 13 shelves = 39 linear feet.

Value (monetary, intrinsic, associational, bibliographic), Rarity, and Provenance
This is a notable rare book collection.

Significance to the Institution / Reason for Preserving Collection
Most of the books were donated by Society founders. The library is known for this collection. The texts are included in a published bibliography, "Hawaiian Language Imprints, 1822 – 1899."

Condition
Varies. Mostly in paper bindings. Paper quality generally good. Some have been rebound at the prison bindery. Most now housed in acid free envelopes and phase boxes.

Use (kind and amount)
Use has grown over the years with the increase in Hawaiian language speakers and scholars and teachers.

For how long should collection be preserved?
In perpetuity.

In what form should collection be preserved (e.g., original, facsimile, new format)?
A few titles have been digitized and posted on the ulukau.org website. Several titles have been reprinted. All formats are important for this collection.

NAME OF COLLECTION
Newspapers Published in Hawai'i

Description
The collection includes newspaper files of more than sixty-four newspapers published in Hawai'i, in English, Hawaiian, and Portuguese languages. The holdings date from 1834 to the 1930s and include original and microfilm copies. These newspapers carried shipping news,

reports of volcanic eruptions, Hawaiian government reports, and Hawaiian genealogies and chants, as well as political, economic, and social news.

A review of the editorial viewpoints of Hawai'i's nineteenth-century newspapers is contained in "Newspapers of Hawai'i 1834 to 1903: From He Liona to the Pacific Cable," by Helen G. Chapin, in The Hawaiian Journal of History, vol. 18, 1984. Published and unpublished guides to the collection are available. Few of these newspapers are indexed.

Newspaper directories include: "Newspapers Published in Hawaii, Survey of the Holdings of the Hawaiian Historical Society," unpublished library guide, 1953; Hawaii Newspapers and Periodicals on Microfilm, A Union List of Holdings in Libraries of Honolulu, compiled by Hawaii State Archives, Hawaii Library Assn., 1977; Hawaiian Newspapers, by Esther K. Mookini, Topgallant Pub., 1974; Hawaii Newspapers, A Union List, prepared by Hawaii Newspaper Project, 1987. This list is a print-out of bibliographic records entered in OCLC.

Newspaper indexes include: Index to marriages and Index to birth notices published in Hawai'i's newspapers 1850–1950, and index to obituaries published in Hawai'i's newspapers, 1836–1950, on microfilm. Selected articles in The Friend are cataloged in the Hawaiian Mission Children's Society card catalog. Published newspaper indexes include: Index to the Honolulu Advertiser and Honolulu Star-Bulletin, 1929– , Office of Library Services, Hawaii Dept. of Education. This index is now available in print form, on microfiche, and on the Hawaii State Public Library on-line public access catalog; The Index to the Maui News 1900–1932, Maui Historical Society, 1985; The Garden Island Index 1971–1980, Kauai Library Assn., 1987; Hawaii Observer Index 1973–1978, Leeward Community College Library, 1978.

Size (number of items) and Volume (linear feet, cubic feet, cabinets, drawers)
Location: newspaper shelves. 4'x3' shelves, 12 feet long. 42 shelves @ 3' = 126 linear feet.

Value (monetary, intrinsic, associational, bibliographic), Rarity, and Provenance
Many newspapers are rare. In some cases HHS has the only copy. These are included in the publication "Guide to Newspapers Published in Hawaii." They also are cataloged in the National Union List of Newspapers.

Significance to the Institution / Reason for Preserving Collection
HHS is known for having this collection. Over the years it has become clear that the original newspapers need to be preserved.

Condition
Mostly very fragile and brittle. Papers published before 1865 are in better condition. Some bound papers are in good condition. Some years of the Hawaiian Gazette have been "silked" to preserve the paper.

Use (kind and amount)
Even though most newspapers have been microfilmed and digitized, researchers still need to refer to the original papers. HHS beginning to scan original newspapers for higher quality digital files.

For how long should collection be preserved?
In perpetuity.

In what form should collection be preserved (e.g., original, facsimile, new format)?
HHS is looking at new technology to scan original papers, OCR, and post on-line, and make microfilm copies from the digital files for a preservation copy.

NAME OF COLLECTION
Manuscript Collections

Description
The manuscript holdings of the Hawaiian Historical Society relate to the Hawaiian Islands and Polynesia. They include letters, journals, diaries, unpublished articles, and research notes. The holdings include original manuscripts, typescripts, and photocopies. The manuscripts are cataloged in the main library catalog by author, title (if available), and subject. Manuscripts are also included in the Society's on-line public access catalog (see the OPAC link on the right).

Important collections include:
- Papers of William D. Alexander (historian, linguist, surveyor), 1890–1912 (250 pieces);
- Journal of Hiram Bingham, Jr. (missionary to Gilbert Islands), 1856–1857, on a voyage from Boston to Micronesia (1 vol.);
- Letters of Sereno E. Bishop (missionary, surveyor, writer) to Gorham D. Gilman (consul general for Hawaiʻi at Boston), 1889–1908 (239 letters);
- Correspondence of George Brown (U.S. consul to Hawaiʻi), 1843–1846 (164 p.);
- Hilo shipping lists by Titus Coan (missionary), 1844–1882 (85 p.);
- Account book of William French (Honolulu merchant), 1818–1819 (1 vol.);
- Sketchbook of Charles Furneaux (artist), an illustrated narrative of the lava flow of 1880–1881 (1 vol.);
- Journals, letters, and notes of Gorham D. Gilman concerning travels in the Hawaiian Islands, 1843–1848 (598 p.);
- Journal and papers of Joseph Jackson (postmaster general), 1856–1859 (1 vol. and 20 pieces);
- Journal of Alexander Liholiho (Kamehameha IV) on a voyage to the United States, England, and France, 1849–1850 (1 vol.);
- Notebooks of William Charles Lunalilo (king of Hawaiʻi), including diaries, letters, and poems, 1847–1853 (110 p.);
- An elementary grammar and vocabulary of the Hawaiian language attributed to Henry Obookiah (pupil at mission school in Cornwall, Conn.), 1817 (1 vol.);
- Private journal of William Cooper Parke (marshal of the Hawaiian kingdom), 1859–1860 (1 vol.);
- Correspondence of Joel Turrill (U.S. consul to Hawaiʻi) with prominent men of the Hawaiian Islands, 1845–1860 (102 items

Size (number of items) and Volume (linear feet, cubic feet, cabinets, drawers)
Location: file drawers, compact shelves, oversize shelves, cubic foot boxes.
File drawers = 18 linear feet. Compact shelves = 24 linear feet. Oversize shelves = 5 linear feet. Cubic ft. boxes = 18.

Value (monetary, intrinsic, associational, bibliographic), Rarity, and Provenance
Mostly unique items, some photocopies. Almost all manuscripts were donated; a few collections were purchased.

Significance to the Institution / Reason for Preserving Collection

This is an eclectic collection. Some important manuscripts, some minor items. All are being cataloged on the HHS OPAC, accessible on the HHS website.

Condition
Mostly good. Housed in acid free folders. Some fragile items have been photocopied for research use.

Use (kind and amount)
Use about the same as the book collection. Many of the manuscripts are cataloged with the book collection in the onsite card catalog.

For how long should collection be preserved?
In perpetuity.

In what form should collection be preserved (e.g., original, facsimile, new format)?
Would be useful to digitize selected collections, i.e. the Stephen Reynolds journal, a 4,000 page typescript.

NAME OF COLLECTION
Photographs of the Hawaiian Islands

Description
The photograph collections contain approximately ten thousand images and two thousand negatives. The largest collection is a General Historical Collection of prints of people, places, and events in Hawai'i's history. The photographs date from the 1860s to the modern period, with the majority being from the 1880s through the 1920s. There are also several small special collections by single photographers, historical postcards, and photograph albums from the late nineteenth and early twentieth centuries. Library subject guides or inventories are available for most of the collections.

The special photograph collections include: The Theodore Kelsey Collection of people and places primarily in the Hilo area in the 1920s; the R. J. Baker Collection, "Persons & Places in Hawaii," 1908 to 1920; the W. H. D. King Collection, "Pictorial Maritime History of Hawaii," depicting sailing ships and steamships that came to Hawai'i; the Robin Kaye Collection, "Lanai Photo Documentary," 1972; and a Micronesian Collection of missionary activities in the Caroline and Marshall Islands, 1897–1898.

The photograph collections also include reproductions of 237 glass-plate photographs made by Dr. Eduard Arning between 1884 and 1886. Arning, a German microbiologist, came to Hawai'i under the sponsorship of King Kalākaua to study leprosy. The Arning photographs are the only large collection from this period to have been meticulously documented to time and place. The originals are in the Hamburgisches Museum für Völkerkunde in Germany.

Size (number of items) and Volume (linear feet, cubic feet, cabinets, drawers)
•6 file cabinet drawers, •1 oversize shelf (glass negs), •14 compact shelves = 37 linear feet, •1 map case drawer (oversize photos)
(6000+ loose b x w photos, 40+ photo albums, 40+ oversize photos, 4x5 copy negs, glass negs, 100+ nitrate negs)

Value (monetary, intrinsic, associational, bibliographic), Rarity, and Provenance

Dates range from 1870s to 1950s. Database of 6,000 images available on website, plus some albums and special collections by photographer. In-house finding aids also available. Considered a small but valued collection by researchers.

Significance to the Institution / Reason for Preserving Collection
This is an important collection to the HHS library. For 10+ years HHS has produced a calendar featuring photos from this collection.

Condition
Generally good. Loose photos housed in mylar sleeves and acid free folders, archival boxes. It has been suggested that photographs in file cabinet drawers be transferred to Hollinger boxes on shelves.

Use (kind and amount)
One of the most used parts of the library collections.

For how long should collection be preserved?
In perpetuity.

In what form should collection be preserved (e.g., original, facsimile, new format)?
Original plus digital.

NAME OF COLLECTION
Maps of Hawai'i and the Pacific

Description
The library has a small collection of nineteenth- and early twentieth-century maps of Honolulu, the Hawaiian Islands, and the Pacific Ocean. The card catalog provides access to the maps in books or cataloged and housed in pamphlet cases. A card inventory lists maps in the map case.

Size (number of items) and Volume (linear feet, cubic feet, cabinets, drawers)
•125 items cataloged on compact shelves, •2 map case drawers, •1 archival newspaper box on newspaper shelves. •1 box of oversize maps rolled & tied, •set of Sanborn Fire Insurance maps on top of file cabinet.

Value (monetary, intrinsic, associational, bibliographic), Rarity, and Provenance
High research value.

Significance to the Institution / Reason for Preserving Collection
This is a small collection, useful to researchers as a byproduct of their research.

Condition
Generally good. Many have been encapsulated or put in plastic sleeves. Map case drawers are overfull. Rolled & tied maps and Sanborn Insurance maps need better housing.

Use (kind and amount)
There is an in-house finding aid for the maps in the map case and newspaper box and researchers find them quite useful, usually as a complement to their research topics.

For how long should collection be preserved?

In perpetuity. Even if maps are digitized, it is useful for researchers to be able consult the actual maps.

In what form should collection be preserved (e.g., original, facsimile, new format)?
Original.

NAME OF COLLECTION
Broadsides Published in Hawai'i

Description
The library has approximately three hundred broadsides published in Hawai'i from 1829 to the early 1900s. These include political and legal notices, election flyers, speeches, social and commercial advertisements, and funeral processions for Hawaiian royalty. A chronological card inventory provides access to the collection.

Size (number of items) and Volume (linear feet, cubic feet, cabinets, drawers)
300 items in 3 map case drawers, plus one broadside scrapbook

Value (monetary, intrinsic, associational, bibliographic), Rarity, and Provenance
An interesting 19th century collection. Many rare items. Most are included in the Hawaiian National Bibliography which has holdings information.

Significance to the Institution / Reason for Preserving Collection
A unique part of the library collection.

Condition
Generally good. Most are encapsulated. The map case drawers are over-full.

Use (kind and amount)
We have only an in-house finding aid. Researchers are usually delighted to find that HHS has them.

For how long should collection be preserved?
In perpetuity.

In what form should collection be preserved (e.g., original, facsimile, new format)?
Original.

NAME OF COLLECTION
Newspaper clipping File

Description
The library has a file of newspaper clippings from the *Honolulu Advertiser* and *Honolulu Star-Bulletin* that was largely assembled in the 1950s and 1960s. The file also includes earlier clippings and printed ephemera and has a sizable biography section covering prominent men and women of Hawai'i. The file is classified by subject according to the Dewey Decimal Classification system.

Size (number of items) and Volume (linear feet, cubic feet, cabinets, drawers)
10 file cabinet drawers. (biography section 4 cabinet drawers, clipping service 1887-1898 one drawer)

Value (monetary, intrinsic, associational, bibliographic), Rarity, and Provenance
Mostly newspaper clippings from Honolulu Star-Bulletin and Honolulu Advertiser. Some ephemera. Assembled by HHS volunteers in the 1950s. Value is mostly nostalgia. Newspapers are indexed from 1929 on and are on microfilm.

Significance to the Institution / Reason for Preserving Collection
Biography section most useful. Still being added to. Clipping Service Bureau articles 1887 – 1898 are of potential use to researchers.

Condition
Newsprint in folders. Okay today but deteriorating over time. Clippings 1887 – 1898 have been photocopied onto acid free paper for researchers to use. The original clippings are stored in archival boxes.

Use (kind and amount)
Not much use. Not directly accessible to researchers. No finding aids. Biography section consulted occasionally. Sometimes very helpful.

For how long should collection be preserved?
Not known.

In what form should collection be preserved (e.g., original, facsimile, new format)?
Can/should collection be digitized?

NAME OF COLLECTION
Pamphlets Published in Honolulu

Description
The library has a large collection of pamphlets published in Honolulu in the nineteenth and early twentieth centuries. These cover a wide range of topics. They are cataloged and shelved with the bound books. In 1968 the Society produced a microfilm edition of pamphlets published during the reign of King Kalākaua. This collection, "Kalakaua's Hawaii 1874–1891," includes forty-six pamphlets dealing with the political, social, and economic history of Hawai'i during the reign of King Kalākaua and the many controversies of the period.

Size (number of items) and Volume (linear feet, cubic feet, cabinets, drawers)
From 1892 to 1951, pamphlets were accessioned separately from the books. The pamphlet accession book has 651 entries. From this point forward, pamphlets were entered with the books. They are cataloged and housed on the shelves along with the book collection.

Value (monetary, intrinsic, associational, bibliographic), Rarity, and Provenance
Unknown.

Significance to the Institution / Reason for Preserving Collection
These are some of the earliest accessions in the library and include rare and difficult to find items. Pamphlets published up to 1900 are included in the Hawaiian National Bibliography.

Condition

These pamphlets are generally fragile. Some are in acid free envelopes in archival pamphlet boxes. Many are still to be rehoused as they are in old acidic envelopes and/or old acidic pamphlet boxes. Many pamphlets are glued into old acidic pamphlet binders. A collection of pamphlets, from HHS and other libraries, was microfilmed in 1968, "Kalakaua's Hawaii, 1874 – 1891." The master negative is stored at the Hawaii State Archives Records Center. HHS has a good positive copy here. Dick Ching of Advanced Micro-Images informed me that the negative is not in good condition. He was able to obtain a scan from the microfilm and provided HHS a copy.

Archival needs
The work of rehousing the pamphlets needs to be completed, transferring them to acid free envelopes and archival pam boxes. The pams in old pam binders may be able to be removed from the binders. Housing the pams in new archival pam boxes will require more shelf space. Shifting the book collection will alleviate this problem.

Access needs
The pamphlets are accessioned and cataloged along with the books in the library card catalog. The catalog information can be transferred to the on-line catalog along with the books.

Use (kind and amount)
These receive the same amount of use as the book collection.

For how long should collection be preserved?
In perpetuity.

In what form should collection be preserved (e.g., original, facsimile, new format)?
One collection of 46 pamphlets has been microfilmed and digitized. Other topical collections could be compiled and microfilmed/digitized.

NAME OF COLLECTION
Journals, Periodicals and Newsletters Relating to Hawai'i and the Pacific

Description
The library has a large collection of periodicals published in Hawai'i, including some in the Hawaiian language published in the nineteenth century. It also collects journals of historical societies of the West Coast and Pacific area, newsletters of historical societies and museums in Hawai'i, and other periodicals that publish articles on Hawai'i and the Pacific.

Size (number of items) and Volume (linear feet, cubic feet, cabinets, drawers)
Periodicals are cataloged and housed on the shelves with the book collection. Some newsletters are on the book shelves, most are in file cabinet drawers. 102+ linear feet of shelf space and 2 file cabinet drawers.

Value (monetary, intrinsic, associational, bibliographic), Rarity, and Provenance
HHS subscribes to or has exchange programs for the periodicals and newsletters. There are complete or nearly complete runs of some periodicals.

Significance to the Institution / Reason for Preserving Collection
They all publish occasional articles on the history of Hawaii. These articles are cataloged in the HHS library main card catalog.

Condition

a) Periodicals no longer published, i.e. *Paradise of the Pacific, Mid-Pacific Magazine*: some runs are in bound sets, some are partially bound, some are in old pamphlet boxes.
b) Periodicals currently being published, i.e. *Oregon Historical Society Quarterly, Journal of the Polynesian Society*: early runs are in bound sets while recent issues are unbound. These are stressed by being squeezed on shelves. There is no room on shelves for continuing issues.
c) Newsletters: some are cataloged and are on the shelves. Most are in two drawers of a file cabinet arranged by title. They have filled up the space allotted. In some cases only the current issue is kept. We have a continuation file, card file, for these newsletters.

Archival needs
Unbound periodicals need to be housed in archival pamphlet boxes and given space on the shelves. Newslettern need to be "weeded".

Access needs
Articles about Hawaii in the early runs of the journals are cataloged in the HHS card catalog. Recent issues are not cataloged by article. There may be on-line indexes for some journals. Otherwise it would be useful to catalog Hawaii articles in recent periodicals and add to the on-line library catalog.
Published indexes to articles are available. The Hawaii Library Association published the *Index to Periodicals of Hawaii* in 1976. David Kittelson compiled *The Hawaiians: an annotated bibliography*, published in 1985. Both of these publications index articles in journals and magazines.
The Hawaiian Journal of History is digitized and available on-line as is the *Journal of the Polynesian Society*. There may be on-line sources for other journals.

Use (kind and amount)
The cataloged articles are called for as often as the books. The other issues don't get any use.

For how long should collection be preserved?
Will printed journal articles become obsolete?

In what form should collection be preserved (e.g., original, facsimile, new format)?
If all the Hawaii articles could be microfilmed/digitized and linked to cataloging records the long runs of journals could be donated to another library.

NAME OF COLLECTION
Oversize Books

Description
Books taller than 11" are placed on the oversize shelves. This shelving is limited and is being filled. Uncataloged oversize books are placed flat on regular shelving, waiting to be cataloged.
The oversize book shelf holds *The Friend* newspapers which are bound, the *Paradise of the Pacific* magaine, most of which are bound, the *Bishop Museum Memoirs*, voyage narrative books, etc. The oversize shelving also holds one shelf of glass plate negatives and one shelf of manuscripts in legal size hollinger boxes.

Size (number of items) and Volume (linear feet, cubic feet, cabinets, drawers)
One end stack of the compact shelving is set up to hold oversize books. It is 67.5 linear feet.

Value (monetary, intrinsic, associational, bibliographic), Rarity, and Provenance
HHS is said to have the most complete run of the *Paradise of the Pacific* magazine.

Significance to the Institution / Reason for Preserving Collection

This is part of the cataloged book collection, a permanent part of the collection.

Condition
Archival needs
More oversize shelving is needed. Some of the serial publications on these shelves are in oversize pamphlet containers. If they are rehoused in more compact containers they can be moved to the regular book shelves.
Access needs
Most oversize books are cataloged. When the compact shelving was set up with new oversize shelves, the catalog cards were not updated for the books moved to these shelves. The shelf card lists were updated. Finding the books now is a two-step process. Updating the cards in the HHS card catalog would be a time-consuming undertaking.

Use (kind and amount)
These items are frequently called for by researchers.

For how long should collection be preserved?
In perpetuity.

In what form should collection be preserved (e.g., original, facsimile, new format)?
The Friend newspaper has been microfilmed and digitized. The *Paradise of the Pacific* magazine has been microfilmed. Volumes 1 and 2 of the *Bishop Museum Memoirs* are digitized and available on the Smithsonian website.

NAME OF COLLECTION
Scrapbooks

Description
The scrapbooks are mostly oversized. They contain newspaper clippings and memorabilia. They have been donated to the Society from various sources.

Size (number of items) and Volume (linear feet, cubic feet, cabinets, drawers)
Approx. 30 scrapbooks are cataloged and kept flat on 4 36" shelves in the book collection.

Value (monetary, intrinsic, associational, bibliographic), Rarity, and Provenance
Several of these scrapbooks are considered "treasures" and are included in the book, "Treasures of Hawaiian History," published by the Society in 1992.

Significance to the Institution / Reason for Preserving Collection
Condition
The scrapbooks are kept flat on the library shelves. Three and one half shelves are allotted to the scrapbooks. They are stacked on top of each other.
Archival needs
The scrapbooks should be put in archival boxes. This will take up more shelf space.
Access needs
Most of the scrapbooks are cataloged. They are designated by an "s" beside the call number. A few are not yet evaluated and processed.

Use (kind and amount)

The cataloged scrapbooks are called for along with the cataloged books.

For how long should collection be preserved?
In perpetuity

In what form should collection be preserved (e.g., original, facsimile, new format)?
The Kilohana Art League scrapbook has been microfilmed, and the Bishop Museum library has a copy. Other scrapbooks could also be microfilmed.

NAME OF COLLECTION
HHS Archives

Description
In 1995, volunteer archivist Susan Campbell organized the Society archives and created a finding aid for them. These are corporate records, correspondence, library records, publication records, grant project records, etc.

Size (number of items) and Volume (linear feet, cubic feet, cabinets, drawers)
The organized archives take up 7 file cabinet drawers.

Value (monetary, intrinsic, associational, bibliographic), Rarity, and Provenance
The records have great value to the institution as they document its history.

Significance to the Institution / Reason for Preserving Collection
These are the unique records of the Society's history dating from 1892.

Condition
Generally good condition. The records have been rehoused in acid free folders. Board meeting minutes are mostly in archival binders. The archives and finding aid need to be updated to include records produced since 1995.

Use (kind and amount)
Mostly staff and board members use the records. Occasionally researchers who are looking for information about people associated with the Society consult them.

For how long should collection be preserved?
In perpetuity.

In what form should collection be preserved (e.g., original, facsimile, new format)?
Original format.

NAME OF COLLECTION
Sheet Music

Description
The sheet music of Hawaiian music is housed in archival boxes on the manuscript shelf. They date from 1867 to the 1960s. They are in polyester sleeves or interleaved with acid free paper. A finding aid was created and is kept up to date as more items are donated.

Size (number of items) and Volume (linear feet, cubic feet, cabinets, drawers)
Approximately 100 items are in this collection which is growing thru donations.

Value (monetary, intrinsic, associational, bibliographic), Rarity, and Provenance
The 1867 sheet music is considered a "treasure" of the Society and is listed in *Treasures of Hawaiian History,* Item #79. Other items are also rare.

Significance to the Institution / Reason for Preserving Collection
Researchers are interested in the history of Hawaiian music.

Condition
Generally good. All the sheet music shows signs of use.

Use (kind and amount)
Occasional use. The finding aid is kept in a binder in the reading room.

For how long should collection be preserved?
In perpetuity.

In what form should collection be preserved (e.g., original, facsimile, new format)?
Original.

SPECIAL COLLECTIONS HOUSED IN MAP CASES

NAME OF COLLECTION
World War II Ephemera and Newspapers

Description
This collection includes *Honolulu Advertiser* and *Honolulu Star Bulletin* (1941 – 1945) newspapers and printed items relating to Hawaii in WWII, including "Speak American" posters, memos to residents, gas ration card, etc. A finding aid for the collection is in a binder in the reading room.

Size (number of items) and Volume (linear feet, cubic feet, cabinets, drawers)
40 items, housed in one map case drawer.

Value (monetary, intrinsic, associational, bibliographic), Rarity, and Provenance
The newspapers are on microfilm. Ephemera has been donated from several sources.

Significance to the Institution / Reason for Preserving Collection
Potential usefulness probably more for exhibit than research.

Condition
Generally good. Newsprint somewhat deteriorated.

Use (kind and amount)
Rarely used.

For how long should collection be preserved?

Collection could be transferred to another library that focuses on WWII

In what form should collection be preserved (e.g., original, facsimile, new format)?
For the ephemera, in original form. Newspapers can be saved for exhibit purposes.

NAME OF COLLECTION
Paintings

Description
The Society owns 5 oil paintings and one ink and wash watercolor. They are hanging in the reading room and the director's office. The oil paintings received conservation treatment at the Pacific Regional Conservation Center, Bishop Museum, in the 1980s. The watercolor was cleaned and re-framed at this time.

Size (number of items) and Volume (linear feet, cubic feet, cabinets, drawers)
6 paintings

Value (monetary, intrinsic, associational, bibliographic), Rarity, and Provenance
Unknown.

Significance to the Institution / Reason for Preserving Collection
They are considered "treasures" of the Society. Reproductions have appeared in many publications.

Condition
The oil paintings are in good condition. The watercolor needs conservation treatment and needs to be moved from its present location or covered due to light degradation.

Use (kind and amount)
The paintings are enjoyed by researchers who come to the library. Reproductions for publication are occasionally requested.

For how long should collection be preserved?
In perpetuity.

In what form should collection be preserved (e.g., original, facsimile, new format)?
If the watercolor can be scanned, a copy can be put on display and the original housed flat in an archival box.

NAME OF COLLECTION
Original Art Works

Description
This is a collection of flat art works consisting of watercolors, political cartoons, lithographs, original drawings, engravings, and architectural drawings.

Size (number of items) and Volume (linear feet, cubic feet, cabinets, drawers)
-Watercolors: 6. -Political cartoons: 12. -Lithographs: 7. -Original drawings: 32. -Engravings: 4. -Architectural drawings: 22. -Paintings on cardboard: 6. All in one map case drawer.

Value (monetary, intrinsic, associational, bibliographic), Rarity, and Provenance
Unknown.

Significance to the Institution / Reason for Preserving Collection
This is a small collection but includes some significant items.

Condition
These items are in polyester film sleeves or acid free folders in acid free map folders in a map case drawer. Several of the items are too large for the map case and are stored on top of the cases, i.e. the Emmert lithographs and the drawings of Queen Emma and her mother Fanny Young.

Use (kind and amount)
Very occasional use. Mostly by researchers looking for images for publications.

For how long should collection be preserved?
In perpetuity

In what form should collection be preserved (e.g., original, facsimile, new format)?
Original. It would be useful to have high res. scans to fill orders for reproductions.

NAME OF COLLECTION
Oversize Illustrations

Description
This collection consists of a "Pictures of Early Hawaii" series, illustrations from various published sources, posters, calendar illustrations, and reproductions of art works. This collection is growing due to continuing donations from a Society member who collects maps and illustrations of Hawaii from published sources, like *Illustrated London News* and *Harper's Weekly*. The finding aid is kept up to date in a binder in the reading room.

Size (number of items) and Volume (linear feet, cubic feet, cabinets, drawers)
One overfull map case drawer and one archival newspaper box.

Value (monetary, intrinsic, associational, bibliographic), Rarity, and Provenance
Not much monetary value but useful to researchers.

Significance to the Institution / Reason for Preserving Collection
Useful to researchers looking for 19th century images of Hawaii.

Condition
Generally good. Housed in polyester film sleeves in acid free map folders.

Use (kind and amount)
Occasional use by researchers looking for images. The most used part of the collection is illustrations from published sources.

For how long should collection be preserved?
In perpetuity.

In what form should collection be preserved (e.g., original, facsimile, new format)?

Would be useful to scan the images for researchers to view online.

NAME OF COLLECTION
Documents & Printed Matter

Description
This collection has documents, newspaper clippings and special issues of newspapers.

Size (number of items) and Volume (linear feet, cubic feet, cabinets, drawers)
-Documents: 9. –Newspapers and clippings: approx. 30 items.

Value (monetary, intrinsic, associational, bibliographic), Rarity, and Provenance
Unknown.

Significance to the Institution / Reason for Preserving Collection
All items relate to 19th century history of Hawaii.

Condition
Varies. Some newspapers in poor condition.

Use (kind and amount)
This collection is rarely used. Items may be useful for exhibits.

For how long should collection be preserved?

In what form should collection be preserved (e.g., original, facsimile, new format)?

NAME OF COLLECTION
CDs, Videos and DVDs

Description
Unorganized collection of various media, some donated, some prepared for HHS, some produced in house. There is no finding aid.

Size (number of items) and Volume (linear feet, cubic feet, cabinets, drawers)
Unknown. Housed on shelf with photo album collection and in director's office.

Value (monetary, intrinsic, associational, bibliographic), Rarity, and Provenance
Unknown.

Significance to the Institution / Reason for Preserving Collection
This collection needs to be organized, a finding aid prepared, and a digital management system set up.

Condition

Use (kind and amount)

For how long should collection be preserved?
Videos no longer playable. CDs and DVDs need to be examined.

In what form should collection be preserved (e.g., original, facsimile, new format)?

NAME OF COLLECTION
Microfilm

Description
Mostly positive microfilm copies of newspapers in the Society's collection. Most microfilm negatives are stored off site at the State Records Center. 19 reels are not newspapers. A finding aid is located next to the microfilm cabinet.

Size (number of items) and Volume (linear feet, cubic feet, cabinets, drawers)
Housed in 8 drawers of a microfilm cabinet.

Value (monetary, intrinsic, associational, bibliographic), Rarity, and Provenance
These films are replaceable.

Significance to the Institution / Reason for Preserving Collection
The microfilms have been very useful in the past, not so much anymore.

Condition
Most reels are not in acid free boxes. Some film dates to the 1950s and is outgassing and deteriorating. These should be disposed of. For long term storage a colder environment is needed.

Use (kind and amount)
Not used much anymore as newspapers are being digitized. "The Index to Births, Marriages, and Obituaries" is the most used in the collection.

For how long should collection be preserved?

In what form should collection be preserved (e.g., original, facsimile, new format)?
If all newspapers and other items are digitized, these use copies will become dispensable.

SUMMARY OF NEEDS AND PRIORITIZED ACTIONS TO MEET THESE NEEDS

Identified Need	Preservation Action	Resources Required	Institutional Priority	Implementation Priority
Environment				
Regularly monitor and record temperature and relative humidity	Assign responsibility for this and continue to monitor and record	Staff time	High	High
Mitigate temperature and humidity fluctuations in vault AND improve conditions in general as much as possible	Work with Mission House staff to adjust environmental systems to accomplish this	Staff time initially; may need to bring in consultants and purchase equipment	High	High
Implement pest management program	Begin pest monitoring and documentation	Staff time initially	High	High
Implement pest management program	Purchase sticky traps and place in storage and processing area as well as reading room	Funds for boards and staff time	High	High
Implement pest management program	Work with HMCS to add weather stripping to front entrance and to caulk and seal all other outside doors	Funds for stripping, caulking and installation	High	High
Implement pest management program	Thoroughly examine all incoming items, particularly	Staff time	High	High

	collections, for pests			
Implement pest management program	Allocate a space for a quarantine room for incoming materials	Staff time	High	High
Implement pest management program	Allow only flowers and plants from professional florists to come in close proximity to collections and continue to restrict potted plants	Staff time	High	High
Improve air quality	Develop regular schedule for changing filters in HVAC system	Staff time and funds for filters	Medium	High
Reduce accumulation of dust in vault	Work with HMCS and HVAC contractor to clean air ducts and improve air filtration by all practical means possible (HEPA air cleaner)	Staff time and funds to hire a contractor and purchase equipment or supplies	High	High
Reduce UV radiation	Work with HMCS to add UV-filtering sleeves to all fluorescent tubes that do not have them	Staff time and funds for additional sleeves	High	High
Ensure that UV filters on fluorescent tubes are effectively monitoring UV radiation	Annually measure UV light levels to ensure that filters are still effective and record date and findings for future reference	Staff time and possibly funds for a light meter if one cannot be borrowed	High	High

Reduce levels of visible light in reading Room	Work with HMCS to install blinds or tinted films OR Reduce bulb wattage in overhead fixtures Or Turn the back row of lights off when not in use	Staff time and funds for blinds, films or new bulbs	High	High
Storage: Facilities and Containers				
Obtain more storage space	Deal with excess copies of books	Funds to hire an appraiser to assess value, set price and arrange for appropriate disposal of excess books	High	High
Obtain more storage space	Hire a space planner or other appropriate person to help make the best use of space	Funds to hire space planner	High	High
Obtain more storage space	Locate adequate off-site storage	Staff time, off-site storage space and boxes for storage of books	High	High
Obtain more storage space	Consider transferring HHS collections that are duplicated in the HMCS library to off-site storage and add a note to the catalog record that the item is in storage and the HMCS copy should be used	Staff time, off-site storage space and boxes for storage of books	High	High

Obtain more storage space	Digitize and transfer all or some of newspaper clipping file to off-site storage	Staff time, off-site storage space and boxes for storage	High	High
Obtain more storage space	Acquire more flat paper storage drawers for maps and similarly-sized items	Funds to purchase drawers and space for drawers	High	High
Obtain more storage space	Create an area for processing and storage of supplies	Funds to hire a space planner or other appropriate person	High	High
Stabilize shelving	Brace with cross bars and fix to walls with strapping	Funds to hire contractor to do this and for necessary supplies	High	High
Get materials off floor	Purchase rolling carts for materials awaiting processing that are currently on the floor	Funds for carts	High	High
Implement a regular schedule of facilities maintenance	Work with HMCS to accomplish this	Staff time	High	High
Remove tripping hazard posed by computer cords and power strips that run through the Reading Room	Hire an electrician to install electric outlets on tables or, at the very least, cover cords with ramp-covers	Funds to hire an electrician and/or supplies	High	High
Begin on-going documentation of building maintenance projects	Work with HMCS to develop a system to document and compile records of all maintenance projects and	Staff time	High	High

	assign someone to maintain this record			
Prevent books in vault from slumping on shelves	Purchase more bookends for stacks	Staff time and funds for bookends	Medium	High
Facilitate safe retrieval of materials on high shelves in vault	Purchase a proper ladder	Funds for ladder	Medium	High
Rehouse items that need this, e.g., newspapers, news clipping files, rolled pieces, oversized materials, pamphlets	Prioritize rehousing projects, identify needed supplies, and begin planning for implementation once there is more space	Staff time initially and funds for supplies later	Medium	High
Consolidate storage of photographs	Consider transferring photographs in file cabinet drawers to Hollinger boxes on shelves with other photographs	Staff time, space on shelves, and funding for boxes	Low	Low
Exhibitions				
Protect Clint watercolor from light damage	Make a facsimile for display, or limit light exposure by covering with light-blocking cloth	Staff time and funds for facsimile or cloth	High	High
Protect Marshall Islands stick	Remove from permanent display if at all possible.	Staff time and funds for vitrines and cloth	High	High

charts from light and other damage	If not possible, put in vitrines to protect them from accidental damage, pests and dust, and cover vitrines with light-blocking cloth.			
Conservation Treatment				
Obtain conservation assessments for collections needing attention	Work with conservators to methodically plan for conservation treatment of collections in need of repair, e.g., books with detached covers in the collection of Early Voyages to Hawaii and the Pacific	Staff time and funding to hire conservators	Medium	High
Obtain conservation assessment for Clint watercolor	Contact a paper conservator	Funds to pay conservator	High	High
Obtain conservation assessment for Kahanamoku painting	Contact a paintings conservator	Funds to pay conservator	High	High
Obtain conservation assessment for the Webber engraved atlases	Contact a book conservator	Funds to pay conservator	High	High
Security and Access				
Protect collections from fire	Discuss with HMCS the possibility of	Staff and board time initially	High	High

	installing adequate fire detection and suppression in HHS			
Protect collections from fire - Ensure that HHS meets local fire codes for safety	Schedule walk-through with local fire marshal; consult with marshal about outdoor grill and cellulose nitrate film	Staff time and funds for upgrades to meet code	High	High
Protect collections from fire - Ensure that fire department is prepared to respond to an emergency at HHS	Provide reliable individuals with floor plans marked with salvage priority locations to keep off-site	Staff time	High	High
Protect collections from water damage	Raise all collections to at least four inches off the floor	Staff time, space and labor to move collections	High	High
Protect collections in event of emergency	Work with HMCS to gather salvage supplies into a marked waterproof container designated for emergency use	Staff time and funds for supplies	High	High
Protect assets financially	Investigate possibility of an insurance plan or self-insured endowment for collections	Staff and board time and funds for insurance/endowment	High	High
Protect digital information from loss	Back up critical electronic records to off-site servers	Funds for off-site electronic storage and staff time	High	High

	or off-site external hard-drives			
Protect digital information from loss	Develop a system to insure that back-ups are made at regular intervals	Staff time	High	High
Protect digital information from loss	Explore options for digital asset management systems	Staff time initially	High	High
Protect cellulose nitrate and cellulose acetate from loss	Decide on a plan of action and implement it	Staff time and perhaps funding depending on action chosen	High	High
Protect cellulose nitrate and cellulose acetate from loss	Consider re-duplicating the nitrate film that has questionable duplicates and disposing of the nitrate through a hazardous waste company or agency	Staff time and funding for duplication and disposal	High	High
Ensure access to collections	Continue processing, cataloging, and inventorying collections	Staff time	High	High
Ensure access to collections	Catalog backlog of books	Staff time	High	High
Ensure access to collections	Store duplicate cataloging records and inventories off-site	Staff time and funds to create microfilm copy for off-site storage	High	High
Ensure access to collections	Check inventories of collections to ensure that no items are missing	Staff time	Medium	High

Improve researchers' access to materials by replacing faulty call number labels with ones that have better adhesives	Investigate what other institutions do and implement a new system	Staff time and funds for new supplies	Medium	High
Improve researchers' access to fragile materials	Obtain a drop-edge copier or scanner	Staff time and funding for the copier or scanner	Medium	High
Improve access to books	Obtain book cradles and other types of supports that are made of inert materials	Staff time and funding for supports	Medium	High
Improve access to books	Expand on-line catalog to include cataloged books	Staff time	High	High
Improve access to books	Consider digitizing all or part of books in collection of Early Voyages to Hawaii and the Pacific for online research use	Staff time and funding	Low	Low
Improve access to collection of Newspapers Published in Hawai'i	Explore new technology to identify a method to produce readable microfilm and digital copies of the originals	Staff time and funding	Low	Low
Improve access to manuscript collections	Consider digitizing selected collections, i.e. the Stephen Reynolds journal	Staff time and funding	Low	Low

Housekeeping				
Maintain cleanliness of stacks	Clean shelves and dust books when shifting collections	Staff time and cleaning supplies	High	High
Maintain cleanliness of stacks	Institute a housekeeping schedule moving forward	Staff time	Medium	High
Maintain overall cleanliness of building	Remove food trash from offices on a daily basis	Facilities staff time	High	High
Formalize all housekeeping procedures	Write out procedures, evaluate and specify cleaning products, train staff in desired cleaning practices, establish a regular schedule, and record everything that is done and when	Staff time	High	High
Policies, Plans and Procedures				
Draft an institutional long-range strategic plan	Develop the outline from the January 2012 meeting into a formal plan	Board and staff time	High	High
Update the preservation plan annually	Set a date for annual review and adhere to it (e.g., beginning of fiscal year)	Staff time	High	High
Expand and complete the emergency plan, adding salvage	Gather information, obtain models from other	Staff time to draft additional information	High	High

instructions, updated vendors and contact lists, shelter-in-place instructions, and forms for reporting incidents and inventory control	institutions and complete plan			
Update the emergency plan annually	Set a date for annual review and adhere to it (e.g., beginning of fiscal year)	Staff time	High	High
Develop a stricter acquisitions policy that is highly selective	Obtain copies from other institutions as models	Staff time to draft policy	High	High
Develop integrated pest management policy	Survey literature on this and obtain models	Staff time to draft policy	High	High
Draft a loan policy that includes environmental requirements	Obtain copies from other institutions as models	Staff and board time to draft policy	Medium	High
Draft a housekeeping manual listing procedures that include stack maintenance and pest management	Obtain models and draft a housekeeping manual	Staff time	Medium	High
Develop a collection management policy	Obtain copies from other institutions as models	Staff time to draft policy	Medium	Medium
Develop a digitization plan to	Hire a consultant to assist with this	Funds to hire a consultant and staff time	High	High

guide projects in a systematic way				
Funding				
Insure stable, on-going funding for conservation	Review library's budget and add a line-item for conservation	Board and staff time and planning	High	High
Secure additional funding for conservation and preservation	Identify appropriate grants, match projects to them, and establish a long-term schedule of regular applications for funding	Staff and board time	High	High
Secure additional funding for conservation and preservation	Seek donor assistance for special purchases	Staff and board time	High	High
Secure additional funding for conservation and preservation	Work with development department and Friends group to raise funds for special projects	Staff and board time	High	High
Staff, Consultants and Training				
Investigate the possibility of student interns	Contact appropriate programs in local colleges and universities	Staff time	High	High
Implement long-range preservation plan	Hire additional staff person (preservation librarian?)	Staff time and funding for position	High	High

| Obtain on-going hands-on training for staff and board members in emergency salvage techniques and response procedures, Red Cross safety classes, the Incident Command System, and other emergency-related topics | Network locally to identify training opportunities | Staff and board time and funding for training | Medium | High |

APPENDICES

LIST OF ACTIONS AND ITEMS REQUIRING FUNDING

Items Needing Funding	Approximate Amount of Funding Needed	Source of Funding	Application or Other Deadline	Pertinent Information
Glue boards/sticky traps	$50.00 per year	Existing grant		
Weather stripping for front entrance and labor to install it	$20.00	Existing grant		
Supplies and labor to caulk and seal entry points of building	$25.00	Existing grant		
Hire HEPA contractor to improve air filtration and reduce dust in building	TBD	Share with HMCS		
Supplies and equipment HEPA contractor needs to improve air quality and reduce dust	TBD	Share with HMCS		
Temperature and relative humidity monitoring equipment if additional equipment is needed	$700.00	Existing grant		PEM2 datalogger

Supplies and labor for HVAC contractor to reposition kitchen exhaust or library air intake	TBD	Share with HMCS		
UV-measuring light meter if one cannot be borrowed locally	$1500.00			
Window blinds or films and lower wattage light bulbs	$75.00	Existing grant		UV filtering sleeves
Supplies and labor to secure shelving in vault	$500.00	Existing grant		
Hire appraiser to deal with duplicates	TBD			
Hire a space planner	TBD			
Additional flat paper storage drawers	$800.00 - $2000.00			Stacking trays or steel drawers
Explosion-proof freezer for cellulosic film	$3000.00			Consider storing elsewhere, UHM
Rolling carts for materials awaiting processing	$300.00			
Rehousing supplies	$5000.00			
Installation of electric outlets on	TBD	Share with HMCS		

tables in Reading Room				
Bookends	$100.00	Existing grant		
Ladder	$500.00			
Facsimile of Clint watercolor???	TBD			
Vitrines and cloth for Stick charts???	TBD			
Hire conservators to carry out conservation treatment assessments and treatments	$10,000.00			
Upgrades to meet fire codes	TBD	Share with HMCS		
Off-site storage for collections' items	TBD			
Off-site storage for duplicate cataloging records and inventories				MOU with UHM
Off-site storage for back-up of critical digital records				MOU with UNM
Insurance plan or self-insured endowment to protect assets financially	TBD			

Duplication of cellulose acetate and nitrate film if decision is made to protect film from loss in this way	TBD			
Salvage supplies	$300.00	Existing grant		REACTPAK®
New call number labeling system and supplies	TBD			
Drop-edge photocopier	$3000.00			
Book cradles and other supports	$200.00	Existing grant		
Cleaning supplies for cleaning books and shelves	$100.00	Existing grant		
Consultant to help draft a digitization plan	TBD			
Additional staff position (preservation librarian)	TBD			
On-going training for staff and board in emergency-related topics	TBD			
Installation of a building-wide fire suppression system	TBD	Share with HMCS		

LIST OF ACTIONS
REQUIRING COLLABORATION WITH THE
HAWAIIAN MISSIONS CHILDREN'S SOCIETY

Action	Resources Required	Priority
Environment		
Mitigate temperature and humidity fluctuations in vault AND improve conditions in general as much as possible	Staff time initially; may need to bring in consultants and purchase equipment	High
Add weather stripping to front entrance and caulk and seal any other points of entry to the building	Funds for stripping, caulking and installation	High
Develop regular schedule for changing filters in HVAC system	Staff time and funds for filters	Medium
Work with HVAC contractor to add HEPA filtration to existing systems or employ portable HEPA air cleaners	Staff time and funds to hire a contractor and purchase equipment or supplies	High
Reduce levels of visible light in reading room by Installing blinds or tinted films OR Reducing bulb wattage in overhead fixtures Or Turning the back row of lights off when not in use	Staff time and funds for blinds, films or new bulbs	High
Storage: Facilities and Containers		
Collaborate with HMCS to obtain more storage space by transferring HHS collections that are duplicated in the HMCS library to off-site storage and adding a note to the	Staff time, off-site storage space and boxes for storage of books	High

catalog record that the item is in storage and the HMCS copy should be used		
Implement a regular schedule of facilities maintenance	Staff time	High
Remove tripping hazard posed by computer cords by hiring an electrician to install electric outlets on tables or, at the very least, cover cords with ramp-covers	Funds to hire an electrician and/or supplies	High
Begin on-going documentation of building maintenance projects by developing a system to document and compile records of all maintenance projects and assign someone to maintain this record	Staff time	High
Security and Access		
Incorporate into the strategic plan a plan for installation of adequate fire detection and suppression in HHS	Staff and board time initially	High
Insure HHS meets local fire codes by scheduling a walk-through with local fire marshal; consult with marshal about outdoor grill and cellulose nitrate film	Staff time and funds for upgrades to meet code	High
Supply fire department with floor plans marked with salvage priority locations	Staff time	High
Housekeeping		
Remove food trash from offices on a daily basis	Facilities staff time	High
Write out procedures, evaluate and specify cleaning products, train staff in desired cleaning practices, establish a regular	Staff time	High

schedule, and record everything that is done and when; develop a Housekeeping Manual		

LIST OF POSSIBLE PROJECTS FOR INTERNS FROM MUSEUM STUDIES PROGRAMS, LIBRARY SCHOOLS OR OTHER RELATED GRADUATE PROGRAMS

Project	Intern	Time Frame	Pertinent Information
Compile a list of local and national grants, with application deadlines, that are appropriate for preservation projects			
Gather information and institutional models to expand and complete the emergency preparedness plan			
Obtain institutional models of loan policies and do research that will facilitate the drafting of a loan policy			
Obtain institutional models of housekeeping manuals, research this topic, and assist staff in drafting a manual			
Write out housekeeping procedures, specifying products and providing record-keeping sheets to include in the manual			
Survey literature on integrated pest management and assist staff in drafting a policy			

Obtain institutional models of collections management policies and gather information for staff to draft this			
Source and price book cradles and supports			
Investigate new call number label systems and source and price materials			
Research, list, source and price salvage supplies			
Source and price vitrines and light-blocking cloth for Marshall Islands stick charts			
Source and price bookends			
Source and price a proper ladder			
Assist staff in developing a system to document and compile records of all maintenance projects			
Source and price rolling carts for materials awaiting processing			
Source and price flat paper storage drawers			
Research, source and price electronic data logging equipment to monitor temperature and relative humidity.			

Index

Page references for figures are italicized.

AAM. *See* American Alliance of Museums
AASLH. *See* American Association for State and Local History
AIC. *See* American Institute for Conservation
ARL. *See* Association of Research Libraries
ATALM. *See* Association of Tribal Archives, Libraries, and Museums
acknowledgments, 2, 12, 49; worksheet for, *51*
action plan and timetable, how to create, 39–45; worksheets for, *40–44*
actions. *See* needs and actions
administrative sanctioning, 19–20
American Alliance of Museums (AAM), 6
American Association for State and Local History (AASLH), 6
American Institute for Conservation (AIC), 7
appendixes, 3, 55
Archives Assessment and Planning Workbook, 6
Assessing Preservation Needs: A Self-Survey Guide, 6
assessment, xi, 3; assistance with, 5–8; by in-house staff, 4–5; by outside consultant, 4; definition of, xii
assessment report. *See* assessment
assistance, sources of, 5–8
Association of Research Libraries (ARL), x
Association of Tribal Archives, Libraries, and Museums (ATALM), 7, 8

Balboa Art Conservation Center, 7
Benchmarks 3.0, 6

CAP. *See* Collections Assessment for Preservation (CAP) survey
CAP survey. *See* Collections Assessment for Preservation (CAP) survey
categories of need, 31–35; list of, *33*; worksheet for, *34*
checklist, 16, *18*
The Conservation Assessment: A Proposed Model for Evaluating Museum Environmental Management Needs, 6
Collections Assessment for Preservation (CAP) survey, xii, 5
Connecting to Collections Care, 8
conservation, definition of, xii
conservation assessment. *See* assessment.
Conservation Center for Art & Historic Artifacts, 7
consultants, 3–5; where to find, 7–8
CoSA. See Council of State Archivists
Council of State Archivists (CoSA), 6

Daniel J. Dial Clock Museum, ix, 24
Darling, Pamela W., 12–13
Description of Collections, 2, 11, 13, 15, 23–24; worksheets for, *25–28*
Digital Preservation Assessment Handbook, 7
Digital Preservation Peer-Assessment, 7
Directory of Archival Consultants, 7

Engle, Cynthia, 61
executive summary, 2, 12, 52–53; worksheet for, *52*

FAIC. *See* Foundation for Advancement in Conservation
FSA. *See* Field Services Alliance
feasibility. *See* prioritizing, criteria for
Field Services Alliance (FSA), 6, 7
Find A Professional, 7

132 / Index

Foundation for Advancement in Conservation (FAIC), 8

GCI. *See* Getty Conservation Institute
Getty Conservation Institute, 6
Grid for Selection of Implementation Priorities, explanation of, 13; worksheet, *14*

HCRR. *See* Humanities Collections and Reference Resources Grants
Hawaiian Historical Society, xi, 3; about plan of, 63–64; plan of, 65–129; using plan, 61–62
Humanities Collections and Reference Resources Grants (HCRR), 5

ICCROM. *See* International Centre for the Preservation and Restoration of Cultural Property
IMLS. *See* Institute of Museum and Library Services
impact. *See* prioritizing, criteria for
implement plan, how to, xi, 57–59
implementation priority, 35–37
indigenous, definition of, xii
Inspire! Grants for Small Museums, 5
Institute of Museum and Library Services (IMLS), 5, 6, 8
institution, definition of, xii
institutional priority, 35–37
Intermuseum Conservation Association, 7
International Centre for the Preservation and Restoration of Cultural Property (ICCROM), 6, 7
introduction, 2, 12, 54–55; worksheet for, *54*

List of Preservation Accomplishments to Date, 2, 12, 47; worksheet for, *48*
Long-Range Action Plan and Timetable, 2, 11, 39–45; worksheets for, *40–44*
long-range preservation plan. *See* preservation plan
LYRASIS, 8

MAP. *See* Museum Assessment Program
methodology, the six steps, xi, 11–12
Midwest Art Conservation Center, 8
Minnesota Historical Society, 3
mission statement, 2, 21
Museum Assessment Program (MAP), 6
Museums for America, 5

NEH. See National Endowment for the Humanities
National Conservation Service, 6

National Endowment for the Humanities (NEH), 5
Native American / Native Hawaiian Museum Services, 5
Native American Library Services: Basic Grants, 5
Native American Library Services: Enhancement Grants, 5
Native Hawaiian Library Services, 5
needs and actions, 11, 29–37; categories of need, 31, *33*; listing, 31–35; prioritizing, 12–15, 35–37; resources needed, 35; schedule, 11, 39–45; worksheets for, *30, 32, 34, 36*
needs assessment. *See* assessment
Northeast Document Conservation Center, 6, 7, 8

Percy, Theresa Rini, xiiin1
PSAP. *See* Preservation Self-Assessment Program
Planning Procedures Checklist. *See* checklist
Preferred Vendors List, 7
preservation, definition of, xii
preservation assessment. *See* assessment
Preservation Assistance Grants, 5
preservation plan, xiii, 1, 19–21; authorship and language, 20; length, 21; preparing final document, 12, 55–56; sections of, 2–3
preservation planning, xi, 1, 11; checklist for, *18*; methodology for, 11–12; using worksheets for, 15–16
preservation process, 1, 11–12
Preservation Planning: Guidelines for Writing a Long-Range Preservation Plan, xi
Preservation Self-Assessment Program (PSAP), 7
A Preventive Conservation Calendar for the Smaller Museum, 6
prioritizing, xi, 11, 12–15; assigning priorities, 13–15; criteria for, 12–13; implementation priority, 15, 35–37; institutional priority, 15, 35–37; using grid for, 13, *14*

RE-ORG Method, 7
risk assessment. *See* assessment

SAA. *See* Society of American Archivists
schedule, 11, 39–45; worksheets for, *40–44*
SHRAB. *See* State Historical Records Advisory Board
STEPS. *See* Standards and Excellence Program for History Organizations
STLPG. *See* State, Tribal, Local, Plans & Grants
Society of American Archivists (SAA), 6, 7
staff support, 19–20

Standards and Excellence Program for History Organizations (STEPS), 6
State Historical Records Advisory Board (SHRAB), 6
Summary of Needs and Prioritized Actions to Meet these Needs, 2, 11; worksheets for, *30, 32, 34, 36*

Table of Contents, 2, 12, 53; worksheet for *53*
The Conservation Assessment: A Proposed Model for Evaluating Museum Environmental Management Needs, 6

timetable. *See* schedule
title page, 2, 12, 49; worksheet for, *50*

University of Illinois Library, 7
updating, 57–58
urgency. *See* prioritizing, criteria for

Williamstown Art Conservation Center, 8
worksheets, xi, 15–16, 24, 29

you, definition of, 7

About the Author

Sherelyn Ogden has more than fifty years of preservation experience as a practicing conservator, consultant, and administrator. She loves teaching and working with the staff of cultural heritage institutions to develop practical solutions to everyday problems. She has consulted widely for libraries, archives, historical societies, museums, and tribal cultural centers and has lectured nationally and internationally. She also enjoys writing and has published extensively. Previous books include *Preservation of Library and Archival Materials: A Manual* and *Caring for American Indian Objects: A Practical and Cultural Guide*.

Sherelyn is a fellow of both the American Institute for Conservation and the International Institute for Conservation of Historic and Artistic Works as well as several other conservation organizations. She has an Master of Arts degree from the Graduate Library School of the University of Chicago and was trained in book and paper conservation at the Newberry Library in Chicago. She held the positions of director of Book Conservation at the Northeast Document Conservation Center, director of Field Services at the Midwest Art Conservation Center, and head of Conservation at the Minnesota Historical Society. She is currently in private practice in Saint Paul, Minnesota, where she continues to treat books and paper, consult, and write about preservation.

www.ingramcontent.com/pod-product-compliance
Lightning Source LLC
Chambersburg PA
CBHW081354230426
43667CB00017B/2834